P9-DDR-051

Table of Contents

Copyright © 2005 SingaporeMath.com Inc., Oregon

Using this Guide

This book is a *guide* for teachers using the Primary Mathematics curriculum. It is designed to help teachers understand the course material, to see how each section fits in with the curriculum as a whole, and to prepare the day's lesson. The course material is divided into 70 sessions. Some sessions include optional games that can also be done during review sessions or in any later session. Sessions can be combined for one day's lesson by spending less time on class participation or discussion or not having as many problems for practice during class time.

This guide is designed to be used with both the U.S. edition and the third edition of *Primary Mathematics*. U.S. conventions and spellings are used in this guide, such as using commas for thousands and colons for time, and not using "and" in writing out whole numbers in words. However, any items specific to either edition, such as different answers, different page numbers, and different exercise numbers, are indicated with a superscript **US** or **3d**.

Workbook exercises can be gone over in class or assigned as homework.

This guide schedules reviews as blocks of several successive sessions. However, you can have a review session every few weeks instead, using selected problems from the textbook and workbook review exercises.

Suggested Material

Number discs

These are discs with 0.001, 0.01, 0.1, 1, 10, 100, 1000, 10,000, and 100,000 written on them. Have some that can be displayed; you can write the numbers on transparent counters if you have an overhead projector. You can also simply draw circles on the board and label them. For student manipulatives, you can write the numbers on opaque counters. Each student or group should have 18 of each type.

Base-10 blocks

A set with unit cubes, rods (10 units), flats (10 rods), and a cube (10 flats). Use ones that can be displayed from the front of the class (such as using an overhead projector or ones that can be stuck onto the board). You can also just draw them on the board.

Number cards

Various number cards for games or group activities, see materials list for each part. You can use index cards, but make sure that the number does not show through the card. Many activities will call for four sets of number cards 0-9 for each group. These can be made from playing cards by removing the face cards, making the Ace a 1, and whiting out the 1 and the symbols for the 10 to make them 0.

Hundreds board

This is a chart with squares in a 10 x 10 array numbered from 1 to 100. Have one that can be displayed, such as one for the overhead projector, or one drawn on the board. You will also need to display a blank hundreds board, or a 10 x 10 array but without numbers in the squares. For students, use laminated or copied hundreds boards with spaces large enough to be covered up by counters, one for each group.

Copyright © 2005 SingaporeMath.com Inc., Oregon

Fraction circles and grids
Displayable circles and grids divided fractional parts.

Counters
Use the opaque round counters that will fit on a hundreds board, or cubes, or any suitable counter. They should be in 4-5 different colors.

Measuring tools
Meter sticks, rulers, protractors, graph paper.

Directional Compass
For finding north.

Connect-a-cubes, multilink cubes, or square tiles.

Number cubes
A cube that can be labeled with different numbers. You need enough for each group of about 4 students to have 2 number cubes.

Measuring tools
Meter sticks, yard sticks, rulers, protractors, set squares (triangles with 90°-45°-45° or 90°-30°-60° angles), graph paper.

Optional Resources

Wiggle Woods CD-ROM

This CD-ROM contains learning activities and two games. The name of the program refers to the bug theme. Topics covered include material from both Primary Mathematics 5 and 6. The following chart correlates the different activities to the appropriate part of *Primary Mathematics 5A*.

Primary Mathematics 5A		*Wiggle Woods Primary Five*
Unit 1 – Whole Numbers	Part 5 – Dividing by Tens, Hundreds or Thousands	Game 1: Level 1
Unit 4 – Area of Triangle	Part 1 – Finding the Area of a Triangle	Area of Triangle
Unit 5 – Ratios	Part 3 – Comparing Three Quantities	Ratios: Activity, Challenge

Copyright © 2005 SingaporeMath.com Inc., Oregon

Supplemental Workbooks

These optional workbooks provide a source of extra problems for more practice, tests, and class discussions. Some have interesting and thought-provoking non-routine problems for discussion.

Extra Practice for Primary Mathematics 5 (U.S. Edition)

This workbook has two to four page exercises covering topics from *Primary Mathematics 5A* and *Primary Mathematics 5B*. The level of difficulty and format of the problems is similar to that of the *Primary Mathematics*. Answers are in the back.

Primary Mathematics Challenging Word Problems 5 (U.S. Edition)

This workbook has word problems only. The problems are topically arranged, with the topics following the same sequence as *Primary Mathematics 5A* and *5B*. Each topic starts with three worked examples, followed by practice problems and then challenge problems. Although the computation skills needed to solve the problems is at the same level as the corresponding *Primary Mathematics*, the problem solving techniques necessary in the challenge section are sometimes more advanced, with the problems requiring more steps to solve. It is a good source, though, of extra word problems that can be discussed in class or of enrichment problems for more capable students. Answers are in the back.

Primary Mathematics Intensive Practice 5A (U.S. Edition)

This supplemental workbook has one set of problems for each topic in *Primary Mathematics*. Each topical exercise has questions of varying levels of difficulty, but the difficulty level is usually higher than that in the *Primary Mathematics* textbook or workbook. Some of the word problems are quite challenging and require the students to extend their understanding of the concepts and develop problem solving abilities. There is also a section called "Take the Challenge!" with non-routine problems that can be used to further develop students' problem solving abilities. Answers are located in the back.

Copyright © 2005 SingaporeMath.com Inc., Oregon

Unit 1 – Whole Numbers

Objectives

- Read and write numbers within 10,000,000.
- Interpret 7-digit numbers in terms of place value.
- Compare and order numbers within 10,000,000.
- Round off numbers to the nearest thousand.
- Use estimation in addition, subtraction, multiplication, and division.
- Multiply or divide by tens, hundreds, or thousands.
- Do mixed operations involving all four operations, with or without parentheses.
- Solve multi-step word problems.

Suggested number of sessions: 19

	Objectives	Textbook	Workbook	Activities
Part 1 : Place Value				**2 sessions**
1	• Interpret numbers within 1,000,000 in terms of place value. • Read and write 6-digit numbers and corresponding number words.	p. 6 p. 7, tasks 1-3		1.1a
2	• Evaluate number patterns involving counting on or back by place value. • Compare and order numbers within 1,000,000.		Ex. 1	1.1b
Part 2 : Millions				**2 sessions**
3	• Understand how big a million is.			1.2a
4	• Read and write 7-digit numbers and corresponding number words. • Compare and order numbers within 10,000,000.	p. 8 p. 9, tasks 1-3 p. 10, Practice 1A	Ex. 2	1.2b
Part 3 : Approximation and Estimation				**3 sessions**
5	• Round whole numbers to the nearest ten, hundred, or thousand.	p. 11 pp. 12-13, tasks 1-7	Ex. 3	1.3a
6	• Estimate the answer in addition and subtraction. • Estimate the answer in multiplication and division of a whole number by a 1-digit number.	p. 13, tasks 8-12	Ex. 4	1.3b
7	• Practice.	p. 14, Practice 1B		1.3c

Copyright © 2005 SingaporeMath.com Inc., Oregon

	Objectives	Textbook	Workbook	Activities
Part 4 : Multiplying by Tens, Hundred or Thousands				**2 sessions**
8	▪ Mentally multiply a 2-digit number by a 1-digit number.			1.4a
9	▪ Multiply a whole number by 10, 100, or 1000. ▪ Multiply a whole number by tens, hundreds, or thousands. ▪ Estimate the answer in multiplication of whole numbers by a 2-digit number.	p. 15 p. 16, tasks 1-8	Ex. 5	1.4b
Part 5 : Dividing by Tens, Hundred or Thousands				**1 session**
10	▪ Divide a whole number by 10, 100, or 1000. ▪ Divide a whole number by tens, hundreds, or thousands. ▪ Estimate the answer in division of whole numbers by a 2-digit number.	p. 17 p. 18, tasks 1-6	Ex. 6	1.5a
Part 6 : Order of Operations				**5 sessions**
11	▪ Mental math			1.6a
12	▪ Do mixed operations involving addition and subtraction without parentheses. ▪ Do mixed operations involving multiplication and division without parentheses.	p. 20, tasks 1-2		1.6b
13	▪ Do mixed operations involving all four operations without parentheses.	p. 19 p. 20, task 3	Ex. 7	1.6c
14	▪ Do mixed operations involving all four operations with parentheses.	p. 20, tasks 4-6	Ex. 8	1.6d
15	▪ Practice.	p. 21, practice 1C		1.6e
Part 7 : Word Problems				**4 sessions**
16	▪ Review part-whole and comparison models for addition, subtraction, multiplication, and division.			1.7a
17	▪ Solve multi-step word problems.	p. 22, tasks 1-2	Ex. 9	1.7b
18		pp. 23-24, tasks 3-4	Ex. 10	1.7c
19	▪ Practice.	p. 25, practice 1D		1.7d

Copyright © 2005 SingaporeMath.com Inc., Oregon

Part 1: Place Values	2 sessions

Objectives

- Read and write numbers within 1,000,000.
- Interpret 6-digit numbers in terms of place value.
- Compare and order numbers within 1,000,000.

Materials

- Number discs (discs with 1, 10, 100, 1000, 10,000, and 100,000 written on them)
- Base-10 set
- Number cards 0-9, 4 sets for each group of students

Homework

- Workbook Exercise 1

Notes

In *Primary Mathematics 4A*, students learned to interpret a 5-digit number in terms of ten thousands, thousands, hundreds, tens, and ones. They also learned to interpret decimals in terms of tenths, hundredths, and thousandths. These are called place values. This is extended here to 6-digit numbers and to the place value of hundred thousands.

The value of a digit is determined by its place in the number. This place-value concept is the basis of the base-10 system of numeration (the Hindu-Arabic system). We use ten digits (0 to 9) to write numbers, with each digit having a value that is ten times as much as the digit in the place to the right of it (and one tenth as much value as the same digit in the place to the left of it). The number 623,456 represents 6 hundred thousands, 2 ten thousands, 3 thousands, 4 hundreds, 5 tens, and 6 ones. The *place value* of the digit 3 is thousands, and its value is 3000.

Students should not have too much difficulty extending place value concepts to these larger numbers. If they do, use concrete manipulatives such as number discs.

Students used number discs in earlier levels, along with a place-value chart. A place-value chart is a table divided into columns or adjacent places for ones, tens, hundreds, thousands, and so on. Number discs can be placed on the place-value chart to represent a number. (Numerals can be used on the place-value chart as well, instead of discs, as on p. 7 of the text.) With discs, 145,136 would look like this:

Hundred Thousands	Ten Thousands	Thousands	Hundreds	Tens	Ones
100,000	10,000 10,000 10,000 10,000	1000 1000 1000 1000 1000	100	10 10 10	1 1 1 1 1 1

Copyright © 2005 SingaporeMath.com Inc., Oregon

When comparing large numbers, students can write the numbers in columns with the digits aligned and then compare the numbers place by place from left to right. They need to be careful to align the place values, not start all numbers at the left. (Most students by now can compare numbers written as a series horizontally by visual inspection and do not need to rewrite them in columns any more.) In the numbers shown at the right, we first compare the ten thousands place. 53,565 is the largest, and 9569 the smallest (with no ten thousands). The others cannot be ordered by the ten-thousands place so we compare the thousands place. 35,198 is second largest. To compare the two remaining numbers, 34,563 and 34,659, we compare the hundreds place. So 53,565 > 35,198 > 34,659 > 34,563 > 9569

34,563
35,198
9,569
53,565
34,659

Note:

In the U.S., a comma is used in the numeral to separate each period of three digits, However, there is an exception; the comma is optional for 4-digit numbers, and the U.S. edition of *Primary Mathematics* does not use it (e.g., 4567 rather than 4,567).
The 3rd edition of Primary Mathematics goes by the European convention of using spaces instead of commas to separate all periods of three digits (e.g., 5 645 136) except for the first one (e.g., 4567 instead of 4 567).

However, when ordering lists of numbers by writing them in columns, as in the example above, it is helpful to add in the comma (or space) for 4-digit numbers if they are being compared to 5-digit numbers.

Numbers like 5,645,136 are written in words as "five million, six hundred forty-five thousand, one hundred thirty-six" in the U.S. (and in the U.S. edition of *Primary Mathematics*). In much of the world, 5,645,136 is written as "five million, six hundred *and* forty-five thousand, one hundred *and* thirty-six". That is, the word "and" is used before the last word (or compound word) in a 3-digit series. In the U.S. however, "and" is no longer used in number words. (The word "and" is now reserved to represent the decimal point.) If you want to use the convention that is in the 3rd edition, adjust the discussion and answers in this guide appropriately.

Copyright © 2005 SingaporeMath.com Inc., Oregon

Activity 1.1a   **Hundred Thousands**

1. Review place-value and introduce the hundred-thousand place.
   - Draw a place-value chart with a column for ones. Draw a 1-disc in the ones column and write 1 below it. You can show them a unit cube from a base-10 set. (The number 1 is being represented in three ways.)
   - Ask students how many digits there are in our number system. (10, if we include 0, which is a place holder and means none). So we write 2 to show two objects, 3 to show three objects, and so on until we get to 9 (draw nine 1-discs and write 9 in the ones column).
   - Ask them how we show the number for one more than 9. Instead of having another digit, we group all ten together and show we have a group of ten ones by creating a place value for tens in order to write how many tens we have (draw another column to the left of the ones column and label it tens, erase the nine 1-discs in the ones column, draw a 10-disc in the tens column, and write 1 below the tens column). Ask students how we show that this one means a ten rather than a one. We have to write a 0 in the ones place to show which place the 1 is in for 10. You can show them a ten-rod from a base-ten set, which represents a ten as a single unit (as does a 10-disc).
   - Add 8 more 10-discs to the tens column and ask for the number represented (90). Erase the 1 under the column and write 9. 90 means we have 9 groups of ten, and no groups of one.
   - Erase the 0 in the ones place and write a 9 there and draw in nine 1-discs in the ones column. Ask students what the number is now (99). Ask them how we show one more. We now have ten ones, which we have to group into a ten (erase the ten 1-discs and draw another 10-disc) but we don't have a digit to show ten tens, so we need another place. Draw a new column to the left, label it Hundreds, erase the ten 10-discs, draw a 100-disc, and write 100 below the columns. You can show students a hundred-flat from a base-10 set.
   - Continue this discussion to create a thousands place (show a thousand-cube from the base-10 set), a ten-thousands place, and then a millions place. Millions will be discussed more in the next session.

   - Refer to **textbook p. 6**. Lead students to see that each cube represents 1000 ones, and each row of ten cubes represents ten thousands. Have students count by ten thousands from ten thousand to a hundred thousand. Since there are 2 layers of hundred-thousands, there are 2 hundred-thousands unit cubes shown here. We write this as 200,000, and the 2 is in the hundred thousands place.
     - Ask students how many ten thousands there are. (20 ten-thousands) 2 hundred thousands = 20 ten thousands
     - Ask how many thousands there are in 2 hundred thousands. (200 thousands) = 200 thousands
     - How many hundreds? (2000 hundreds) = 2000 hundreds
     - How many tens? (20,000 tens) = 20,000 tens
     - How many ones? (200,000 ones) = 200,000 ones

2. Discuss 6-digit numbers. Use number discs and a place-value chart.
   - Draw some discs on the chart and have students write and say the number.
   - Point out that we write a comma for each set of 3 numbers from the right. A set of three numbers is called a period. We have 3 place values that are for *ones*, *tens*, and *hundreds*, and then three place values that are for *one* thousand, *ten* thousand, and *hundred* thousand. We read the number in groups of three. So 456,456 is read as four hundred fifty-six *thousand*, four hundred fifty-six.

Copyright © 2005 SingaporeMath.com Inc., Oregon

- Write the numbers in words. Point out that we write a comma after we say thousand.
- Ask for the value of various digits. For example, in 456,456 there is a digit 5 in the ten-thousands place, with a value of 50,000, and a digit 5 in the tens place, with a value of 50.
- Write the number as the sum of the values of each digit.

$$456,456 = 400,000 + 50,000 + 6000 + 400 + 50 + 6$$

- Repeat with a number where 0 is used as a place-holder.

$$204,006 = 200,000 + 4000 + 6$$

3. Have students do **tasks 1-3, textbook p. 9**.

Activity 1.1b   **Number patterns**

1. Find numbers where the value of the digit in one place is increased or decreased by 1, 2 or 3.
   - Write a 6-digit number. Ask students for the number that is 1, 2, or 3 x 1, 10, 100, 1000, 10,000, or 100,000 more or less than the given number.

     $$531,\underline{6}95 + \underline{3}00 = 531,995$$

     $$\underline{6}31,495 - \underline{1}00,000 = 531,495$$

     - Write the corresponding equations. Underline the digits that are being increased or decreased in both numbers to emphasize the placement of the digits.

     $$1\underline{2}0,495 - \underline{3}0,000 = 90,495$$

     - Students can count on or count back in that place value, including the next higher place (or lower) place value when necessary. For example, with 120,495 – 30,000 they need to count back from 12 ten thousands: 11 ten thousands, 10 ten thousands, 9 ten thousands.

     $$24\underline{9},495 + \underline{1}000 = 250,495$$

   - Write a number sequence with a missing term where one of the place values increases or decreases by 1, 2, or 3 and have students determine the missing term.

     236,567   238,567   _____   242,567

2. Create number patterns.
   - Have students work in pairs. One student creates a number pattern and the other gives the next item in the sequence. Students switch roles after each pattern completion.

3. Compare and order numbers within 1,000,000.
   - Write two 6-digit numbers on the board, such as 423,987 and 423,879.
   - Call on a student to tell you which is larger. Ask the student to explain why it is larger.
   - Write one number below the other, lining the digits up. Remind students that we first compare the digits in the highest place. If one is larger, then that entire number is larger. If they are equal, then we compare the digit in the next smaller place and so on until we get to two digits in the same place that are different.

     4 2 3, 9 8 7
     4 2 3, 8 7 9

   - Write a list of at least four different numbers within 1,000,000 on the board and have students put them in order from smallest to largest.

Workbook Exercise 1

Copyright © 2005 SingaporeMath.com Inc., Oregon

Part 2: Millions	**2 sessions**

Objectives

- Understand how big a million is.
- Read and write 7-digit numbers and corresponding number words
- Compare and order numbers within 1,000,000.

Materials

- Number discs (discs with 1, 10, 100, 1000, 10,000, and 100,000 written on them)

Homework

- Workbook Exercise 1

Notes

In this section students will work with numbers up to 10 million only.

You may want to introduce larger numbers at this time as an optional activity.

Numbers are arranged in groups of three places called periods. The places within periods repeat (hundreds, tens, ones). Commas are used in the U.S. to separate periods. The names for numbers larger than a million are based on the number of 000's after 1 thousand and prefixes. For example:

bi = 2 — a billion has two sets of ,000's after a thousand
tri = 3 — a trillion has three sets of ,000's after a thousand
quad = 4 — a quadrillion has four sets of ,000's after a thousand
quint = 5 — a quintillion has five sets of ,000's after a thousand
sext = 6 — a sextillion has six sets of ,000's after a thousand

The European system is different after eight 0's, or after a hundred million.
In particular, a billion is 10^9 = 1,000,000,000 in the American system and 10^{12} = 1,000,000,000,000 in the European system. For 10^9, Europeans say "thousand million" or "milliard." In more recent years, the "American" system has become widely used in England as well as in the United States.

million	1,000,000
ten million	10,000,000
hundred million	100,000,000
billion [thousand million or milliard]	1,000,000,000
trillion [billion]	1,000,000,000,000
quadrillion [billiard]	1,000,000,000,000,000
quintillion [trillion]	1,000,000,000,000,000,000
sextillion [trilliard]	1,000,000,000,000,000,000,000
septillion [quadrillion]	1,000,000,000,000,000,000,000,000
octillion [quadrilliard]	1,000,000,000,000,000,000,000,000,000
nonillion [quintillion]	1,000,000,000,000,000,000,000,000,000,000
decillion [quintillard]	1,000,000,000,000,000,000,000,000,000,000,000

Copyright © 2005 SingaporeMath.com Inc., Oregon

One googol is a ONE followed by 100 zeros.
One googolplex is a 1 followed by googol number of zeros.

There are about 2 billion seconds in an average life time.
There are about 6 billion people on earth.
There are about 50 trillion cells in an average human being.
There are about one quadrillion grains of sand on a beach.
There are about a sextillion cups of water in the ocean.
US: The earth weighs about one septillion pounds.
US: The sun weighs about one nonillion pounds.

Activity 1.2a   **Millions**

1. Develop an idea for the size of a million.
   - Ask students what follows 999,999. It is 1,000,000, 1 million. We have to create another place value, which is called the millions place.
   - Refer back to **textbook p. 6**. A million unit cubes would be a cube that is ten layers of 10 by 10 thousand cubes.
   - Discuss or have your student do some activities to help them gain an idea about large numbers like a million. Help your student with calculations that involve division by 3 or 4 digit numbers.

   ➢ How many liters are a million drops of water? Use an eye dropper and a medicine spoon and count the number of drops in a milliliter. There are about 20 drops in a milliliter. Multiply by 1000 to get the number of drops in a liter, and divide 1,000,000 by this number to get the number of liters. A million drops is about 50 liters.

   ➢ How long would it take to count to a million, if you counted at the rate of one number per second? There are 60 seconds in a minute, 3600 seconds in an hour, and 86,400 seconds in a day. Divide 1,000,000 by 86,400. It takes about 12 days.

   ➢ How big a square would a million unit-cubes from a base-10 set make? You would need 1000 rows of 1000 squares. 1000 cm is 10 meters. So the square would be 10 meters on a side.

   ➢ If you could live a million days, how old would you be? Divide 1,000,000 by 365 days and the answer is about 2740 years old.

   ➢ (U.S) How high would a stack of a million pennies be? Measure a stack of pennies. There are 16 pennies in an inch, 192 pennies in a foot, 192 x 5280 = 1,013,760 pennies in a mile. So a stack of a million pennies would be about a mile high.

   ➢ (U.S) If pennies were laid side by side, how long would a row of a million pennies be? Put pennies side by side until they are a foot long. There are 5280 feet in a mile. There are 16 pennies side by side in a foot, and 84,480 in a mile. Divide 1,000,000 by 84,480. A million pennies side by side would be about 12 miles long.

   ➢ (U.S) How much do one million pennies weigh? 1 penny weighs about one tenth of an ounce. So there are 160 pennies in a pound. Divide 1,000,000 by 160. A million pennies weigh about 6250 pounds (about 3.12 tons). Or, there are about 353 pennies per kilogram. (160 pennies/lb ÷ 0.454 kg/lb) So a million pennies weigh about 2800 kilograms, about the weight of a half-grown elephant.

Copyright © 2005 SingaporeMath.com Inc., Oregon

Activity 1.2b   **Practice**

1. Discuss **textbook p. 8** and **tasks 1-3, textbook p. 9**.

2. Have students do **Practice 1A, textbook p. 10**.

3. Practice writing and comparing numbers within 1,000,000
   - Have students work in groups. Provide each group with 4 sets of number cards 0-9.
     Cards are shuffled. Each student selects 7 cards and lays them next to each other to
     form a 7-digit number. The student then writes the number down in numerals and
     words. Students compare their numbers and list them in order.

4. Game

   Material: Number cards 0-9, one more set than the number of players.

   Procedure: Each player draws 7 lines on paper for the places for a 7-digit number. Players
   take turns drawing cards and writing the number drawn on one of the lines. Once the digit
   has been written it must stay in that place. After all players have drawn 8 cards, they
   compare their numbers. The one with the highest number wins. The players are allowed to
   see each other's number. They can apply some strategy to determine what numbers are
   likely to remain and what their chances are of drawing a high number to put in the highest
   place.

Workbook Exercise 2

Part 3: Approximation and Estimation	**3 sessions**

Objectives

- Round off whole numbers to the nearest thousand.
- Estimate the answer to addition, subtraction, multiplication, and division problems.

Materials

- Number lines

Homework

- Workbook Exercise 5
- Workbook Exercise 6
- Workbook Exercise 7

Notes

In Primary Mathematics 4, students learned to round off numbers to the nearest ten or to the nearest 100. This will be reviewed here and extended to rounding off numbers to the nearest thousand.

A number is rounded off to the ten, hundred, or thousand it is nearest to. By convention, if a number is exactly halfway between two consecutive tens or hundreds, it is rounded to the higher ten or hundred.

In the same way, to round off a number to the thousand, we look at the digit in the hundreds place. If it is 5 or more, we round up to the next thousand. If it is smaller than 5, we round down.

The symbol " $\approx$ " is used to mean "is about" or "is approximately".

$$123{,}456 \approx 123{,}000$$
$$156{,}502 \approx 157{,}000$$
$$237{,}500 \approx 238{,}000$$

Throughout *Primary Mathematics*, we work to make sure that students understand what they are doing, and why. As part of this, we expect students to develop the habit of checking whether an answer is reasonable: and if not, to go back over the problem and their calculation. For this reason, estimation is a strong tool for the teacher as well as for the student.

Students should round to numbers which are easy to perform mental calculations with. In addition and subtraction, they should generally round the smallest number to one non-zero digit, and then the larger number to the same place.

$$
\begin{array}{cc}
6326 + 4608 \\
\downarrow \quad\ \downarrow \\
6000 + 5000 = 11{,}000
\end{array}
$$
Both digits are rounded to the thousands place.

$$
\begin{array}{cc}
48{,}943 + 392 \\
\downarrow \quad\quad \downarrow \\
48{,}900 + 400 = 49{,}300
\end{array}
$$
Since 392 is rounded to 400 to get a number with one non-zero digit, round 48,943 to the nearest hundred.

Copyright © 2005 SingaporeMath.com Inc., Oregon

By now, a student should be able to mentally add 1-digit to any place in a number (e.g. 3456 + 80 or 3456 + 900) and to mentally subtract 1-digit from any place in a number (e.g. 1234 – 80 or 1234 – 900). If your students are unable to do this, you may need to review from the following levels:

➢ *Primary Mathematics 3B*, Unit 1 and accompanying sections in *Primary Mathematics 3B Teacher's Guide*
➢ *Primary Mathematics Teacher's Guide 4A*, Activities 1.1e and 1.1f

When rounding to estimate the answer in multiplication by a 1-digit number, round the larger number to a number with one non-zero digit, unless it is easy to mentally multiply more than one non-zero digit with the single digit.

4592 x 9	2319 x 3	24,516 x 3
↓	↓	↓
5000 x 9 = 4500	2300 x 3 = 6900	25,000 x 3 = 75,000

In the second and third example, it should be easy for the students to multiply 23 x 3 or 25 x 3 (3 quarters) mentally. The estimated answer will be closer to the actual answer. However, they can also round to 2000 x 3 or 20,000 x 3, and the answer will tell the student the correct number of places that the actual answer should have.

In rounding numbers to estimate the answer to the division of 4-digit number by a 1-digit number, we round to the nearest multiple of the single digit, not necessarily to the nearest thousand.

$$3810 \div 6$$
$$\downarrow$$
$$3600 \div 6 = 600$$

Rounding to 4000 would result in 4000 ÷ 6, which is not easy to calculate mentally.

In *Primary Mathematics 3A*, students learned to multiply tens, and hundreds, by a 1-digit whole number. This was reviewed in *Primary Mathematics 3B*. If necessary, review using *Primary Mathematics 3B*, Unit 1 and accompanying sections in *Primary Mathematics 3B Teacher's Guide*.

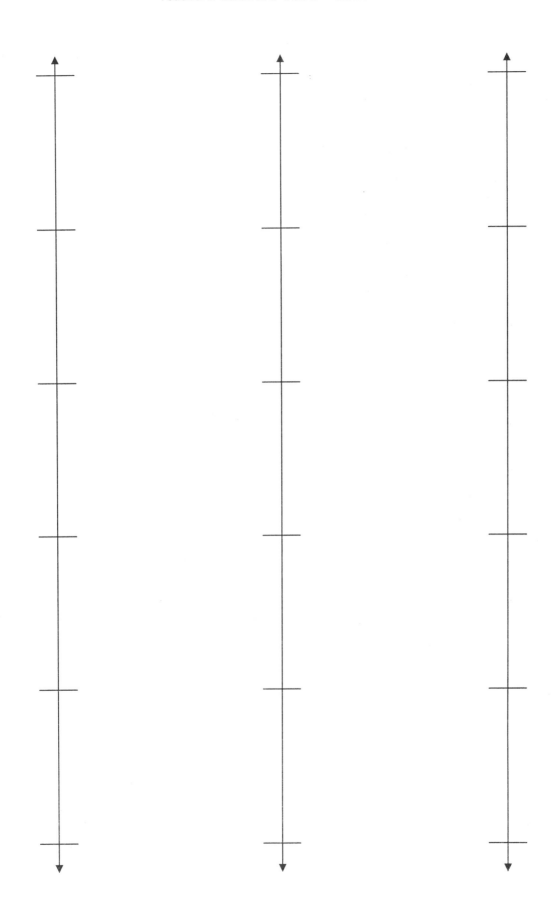

Copyright © 2005 SingaporeMath.com Inc., Oregon

Activity 1.3a   **Round whole numbers**

1. Round to the nearest 10.
   - Provide students with a copy of the blank number lines on the previous page. Have them mark consecutive tens on the first one. Then have them mark a number between two consecutive tens by estimating where it should go. They should be able to determine that 3458, for example, would be close to 3460.

   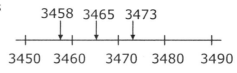

   $$3458 \approx 3460$$
   $$3465 \approx 3470$$
   $$3473 \approx 3470$$

   - Remind students that when we round off a number to the nearest ten, we want a number with 0 in the ones place.
   - To round a number to the nearest ten, we look at the digit in the ones place. If it is 5 or more, we round up, that is, we add 1 to the digit in the tens place. If it is less than 5, we round down; that is, we keep the digit in the tens place the same. In both cases, we replace the digit in the ones place with 0.
   - Tell students we use a squiggly equal sign to mean "is about" or "is approximately".

2. Round to the nearest 100.
   - Repeat the last activity using the second number line, but have students mark off consecutive hundreds and then mark numbers between two consecutive hundreds.
   - Then have students round the number to the nearest 100.
   - Include examples such as $45,975 \approx 46,000$ or $45,032 \approx 45,000$. Ask them what 45 rounded to the nearest 100 would be. (0)
   - To round a number to the nearest hundred, we look at the digit in the tens place. If it is 5 or more, we round up, that is, we add 1 to the digit in the hundreds place. If it is less than 5, we round down; that is, we keep the digit in the hundreds place the same. In both cases, we replace the digits in the tens and one places with 0.

3. Round to the nearest 1000.
   - Repeat the first activity using the third number line, but have students mark off consecutive thousands, locate a number between two consecutive thousands, and then round the number to the nearest thousand. Include an example such as $49,975 \approx 50,000$.

   $$6\,5\,2,\underline{4}\,3\,2 \rightarrow 652,000$$
   less than 5

   $$6\,5\,1,\underline{5}\,0\,2 \rightarrow 652,000$$
   5 or more

   - To round a number to the nearest thousand, we look at the digit in the hundreds place. If it is 5 or more, we round up, that is, we add 1 to the digit in the thousands place. If it is less than 5, we round down; that is, we keep the digit in the thousands place the same. In both cases, we replace the digits in the hundreds, tens, and ones places with 0.

4. Discuss **textbook p. 11**
   - Be sure your students can interpret the divisions on these first number lines. For the first number line, each division is 10. So the first division after 4850 is 4860, and the next one is 4870. 4865 is between 4860 and 4870 and so falls on the number line between these two divisions. Ask students to locate some other numbers between 4800 and 4900 on the number line, such as 4876, and determine whether they are nearer to 4800 or 4900.

Copyright © 2005 SingaporeMath.com Inc., Oregon

- Ask students to determine the divisions on the second number line. Each division is now 100. Ask students to locate some other numbers as well and round them to the nearest thousand.

5. Have students do **tasks 1-7, textbook pp. 12-13**.

Workbook Exercise 3

Activity 1.3b   **Estimate answers**

1. Discuss **tasks 8-9, textbook p. 13**.
   - If necessary, spend an extra session or more reviewing mental math techniques using material from *Primary Mathematics 3B*, Unit 1 and accompanying sections in *Primary Mathematics 3B Teacher's Guide* and from *Primary Mathematics Teacher's Guide 4A*, Activities 1.1e and 1.1f. A brief review is given here. Further review can also be done during the next session (activity 1.3c).
   - Write the following problems, and discuss ways to find the sum or difference.

     ➢ 345 + 6 = 351
       Adding 5 and 6 increases the tens. Write down the hundreds (3) then the tens + 1 (5), then the ones resulting from 5 + 6.
     ➢ 34,500 + 600 = 35,100
       Add in the same way as 345 + 6. Now we are adding 345 hundreds + 6 hundreds, so the answer is hundreds
     ➢ 345 – 6 = 339
       Since 5 is less than 6, the tens must be decreased by 1. Write down the hundreds (3), then the tens – 1 (3), then the ones for either 15 – 6 or 3 + 6.
     ➢ 34,500 – 600 = 33,900
       Subtract in the same way as for 346 – 6, but now we are subtracting hundreds, so add 2 more 0's to the answer for hundreds.

   - Remind students that when we multiply a single digit number by a number that is a digit with 0's following it, we can take off the trailing 0's, multiply, and then add the trailing 0's back on. So 9 hundreds x 4 is the same as 9 x 4 except that the answer is 36 hundreds instead of 36 ones.

     900 x 4 = 9 hundreds x 4 = 36 hundreds = 3600
     5000 x 8 = 5 thousands x 8 = 40 thousands = 40,000

   - We can do the same thing when dividing by a 1-digit number, as in:

     3600 ÷ 9 = 36 hundreds ÷ 9 = 4 hundreds = 400

   - However, when we take off the trailing 0's, we want a number that is a multiple of the number we are dividing by, so we may need to leave one of the 0's on, as in:

     30,000 ÷ 6 = 30 thousands ÷ 6 = 5 thousands = 5000

2. Discuss finding the estimate in addition and subtraction problems.
   - Remind students that it is useful to quickly find an approximate answer to a math problem in order to get an idea of what the actual answer should be. If we then find the exact answer and it is considerably different from our approximate answer, then we know we made a mistake in the computation. When we find an approximate answer, we are making an **estimate**.

Copyright © 2005 SingaporeMath.com Inc., Oregon

- Write an addition expression, such as 4573 + 8652. Have students round off each term and then add to find an estimate. Then have students find the exact answer and compare it to their estimate.

$$4573 + 8652$$
$$\downarrow \qquad \downarrow$$
$$5000 + 9000 = 14{,}000 \text{ rounded}$$
$$4573 + 8652 \approx 14{,}000 \text{ approximate}$$
$$4573 + 8652 = 13{,}225 \text{ exact}$$

- Repeat with a subtraction problem.

$$7014 - 2871$$
$$\downarrow \qquad \downarrow$$
$$7000 - 3000 = 4000 \text{ rounded}$$
$$7014 - 2871 \approx 4000 \text{ approximate}$$
$$7014 - 2871 = 4143 \text{ exact}$$

- Repeat with some problems where one of the terms is a 5-digit or 6-digit number and the other a 4-digit number, such as 32,914 + 4790. Students should round to the nearest thousand. Tell them that we generally round the smaller number so that there is one non-zero digit, and then round the larger number to the same place. We then find the sum or difference using the same strategies for finding the sum or difference of a 1-digit number and a number with more digits. (e.g., find 48 + 3 to find 48 hundreds + 3 hundreds).

$$32{,}914 + 4790$$
$$\downarrow \qquad \downarrow$$
$$33{,}000 + 5000 = 38{,}000 \text{ rounded}$$
$$32{,}914 + 4790 \approx 38{,}000 \text{ approximate}$$
$$32{,}914 + 4790 = 37{,}704 \text{ exact}$$

3. Discuss estimation in multiplication.
   - Ask students to round 4576 to the nearest thousand. Then ask them to multiply the rounded-up number (5000) by 4. Remind them that this gives an estimate of the actual answer. An estimate helps us to check that our actual answer has the correct number of places. (This is particularly useful when multiplying by 2-digit numbers or a decimal).
   - You can have them find the actual answer.

$$4576 \times 4$$
$$\downarrow$$
$$5000 \times 4 = 20{,}000 \text{ rounded}$$
$$4576 \times 4 \approx 20{,}000 \text{ approximate}$$
$$4576 \times 4 = 18{,}304 \text{ exact}$$

4. Discuss estimation in division
   - Remind students that we can also round to estimate the answers to division problems, but instead of rounding to a number with only one non-zero digit, we round to a number where the first 2-digits are a multiple of the digit we are dividing by. Ask them how they would round 4608 to estimate the answer to 4608 ÷ 3. We don't round to 5000, because 5000 ÷ 3 is not easy to compute mentally. So instead we round to 6000.
   - We could also round to 4500, if we remember that 3 x 15 = 45. This would give us a closer estimate.

$$4608 \div 3$$
$$\downarrow$$
$$6000 \div 3 = 2000 \text{ rounded}$$
(6 is a multiple of 3)
$$4608 \div 3 \approx 2000 \text{ approximate}$$
$$4608 \div 3 = 1536 \text{ exact}$$

5. Discuss **tasks 10-12, textbook p. 13**

Workbook Exercise 4

Activity 1.3c   **Practice**

1. Use **Practice 1B, textbook p. 14** to review topics covered so far.

Copyright © 2005 SingaporeMath.com Inc., Oregon

Part 4: Multiplying by Tens, Hundreds or Thousands	2 sessions

Objectives

- Multiply a whole number by 10, 100, or 1000.
- Multiply a whole number by tens, hundreds, or thousands.
- Multiply tens, hundreds, or thousands by each other.
- Estimate the answer in the multiplication of a whole number by a 2-digit number.

Materials

- Number discs (discs with 1, 10, 100, 1000, 10,000 and 100,000 written on them)

Homework

- Workbook Exercise 5

Notes

In *Primary Mathematics 4A*, students learned to mentally multiply a 2-digit number by tens, and to multiply tens, hundreds, and thousands by a 1-digit whole number. They also learned to estimate the answer when multiplying a 3-digit number by a 2-digit number. These concepts are extended to multiplying whole numbers of up to 4-digits by tens, hundreds, or thousands. The strategy simply involves adding on the correct number of 0's. This skill is used in estimating when multiplying numbers of more than 1-digit by each other. Since estimation is used to help determine whether the actual answer to a problem is reasonable in terms of place value, it is important for the student to be able to estimate competently.

To multiply a number by 10, 100, or 1000, we can obtain the answer by simply adding the correct number of 0's to the number.

To multiply a number by tens, we can do it in two steps. We first multiply by the digit in the tens place, add a 0 to the product.

Students can find 45 x 3 mentally or use the multiplication algorithm, and then add a 0

$$45 \times 30$$

$$45 \xrightarrow{\times 3} 135 \xrightarrow{\times 10} 1350$$

$$\begin{array}{r} 4\ 5 \\ \times\ \ \ 3\ \mathbf{0} \\ \hline 1\ 3\ 5\ \mathbf{0} \end{array} \quad \text{or} \quad \begin{array}{r} 4\ 5 \\ \times\ \ \ 3\ 0 \\ \hline 1\ 3\ 5\ \mathbf{0} \end{array}$$

To multiply a number by hundreds or thousands, we can also do it in two steps:

$$86 \times 200$$

$$86 \xrightarrow{\times 2} 172 \xrightarrow{\times 100} 17{,}200$$

$$\begin{array}{r} 8\ 6 \\ \times\ \ \ 2\ \mathbf{0}\ \mathbf{0} \\ \hline 1\ 7\ 2\ \mathbf{0}\ \mathbf{0} \end{array} \quad \text{or} \quad \begin{array}{r} 8\ 6 \\ \times\ \ \ 2\ 0\ 0 \\ \hline 1\ 7\ 2\ \mathbf{0}\ \mathbf{0} \end{array}$$

$$71 \times 9000$$

$$71 \xrightarrow{\times 9} 639 \xrightarrow{\times 1000} 639{,}000$$

$$\begin{array}{r} 7\ 1 \\ \times\ \ 9\ \mathbf{0}\ \mathbf{0}\ \mathbf{0} \\ \hline 6\ 3\ 9\ \mathbf{0}\ \mathbf{0}\ \mathbf{0} \end{array} \quad \text{or} \quad \begin{array}{r} 7\ 1 \\ \times\ \ 9\ 0\ 0\ 0 \\ \hline 6\ 3\ 9\ \mathbf{0}\ \mathbf{0}\ \mathbf{0} \end{array}$$

Copyright © 2005 SingaporeMath.com Inc., Oregon

To multiply tens, hundreds, or thousands with each other, we take off trailing 0's, multiply the numbers together, and then add the trailing 0's from both numbers back on.

$$34\mathbf{00} \times 6\mathbf{000}\ \begin{aligned} &= 34 \times 100 \times 6 \times 1000 \\ &= 34 \times 6 \times 100 \times 1000 \\ &= 204 \times 100 \times 1000 \\ &= 20400 \times 1000 \\ &= 20{,}4\mathbf{00{,}000} \end{aligned}$$

$$5\mathbf{000} \times 8\mathbf{000} = 40{,}\mathbf{000{,}000}$$

Students need to be competent in multiplication facts.

Students who have used prior levels of Primary Mathematics can probably multiply 2-digit numbers by a 1-digit number mentally, as well as by using the multiplication algorithm. This is covered in Activity 1.4a. The mental math worksheet on the next page is for Activity 1.4a. Answers are given here:

Mental Math 1

1. 231
2. 150 + 20 = 170
3. 160 + 14 = 174
4. 240 + 18 = 258
5. 320 + 40 = 360

6.	425	21.	384
7.	434	22.	141
8.	165	23.	124
9.	258	24.	552
10.	252	25.	84
11.	184	26.	738
12.	168	27.	196
13.	180	28.	252
14.	639	29.	249
15.	84	30.	135

Copyright © 2005 SingaporeMath.com Inc., Oregon

Mental Math 1

1. 77 x 3 = 210 + 21 = _____

2. 34 x 5 = _____ + _____ = _____

3. 87 x 2 = _____ + _____ = _____

4. 43 x 6 = _____ + _____ = _____

5. 45 x 8 = _____ + _____ = _____

6. 85 x 5 = _____   16. 64 x 6 = _____

7. 62 x 7 = _____   17. 47 x 3 = _____

8. 33 x 5 = _____   18. 31 x 4 = _____

9. 43 x 6 = _____   19. 69 x 8 = _____

10. 63 x 4 = _____   20. 28 x 3 = _____

11. 23 x 8 = _____   21. 82 x 9 = _____

12. 56 x 3 = _____   22. 49 x 4 = _____

13. 36 x 5 = _____   23. 36 x 7 = _____

14. 71 x 9 = _____   24. 83 x 3 = _____

15. 21 x 4 = _____   25. 27 x 5 = _____

Copyright © 2005 SingaporeMath.com Inc., Oregon

Activity 1.4a   **Mental Multiplication**

1. Discuss mental multiplication of a 2-digit number by a 1-digit number.

   - Show your students how multiplication of a 2-digit number by a 1-digit number can be done mentally by splitting the 2-digit number into tens and ones, first multiplying the tens, then the ones, and adding the two partial products together. If the student can remember and add the partial products mentally, then the whole problem can be done mentally.

        52×4

        $$\begin{array}{r} 50 + 2 \\ \times \qquad 4 \\ \hline 200 + 8 \; = \; 208 \end{array}$$

        47×3

        $$\begin{array}{r} 40 + 7 \\ \times \qquad 3 \\ \hline 120 + 21 \; = \; 141 \end{array}$$

   - We can also calculate 39×5 mentally as $40 \times 5 - 5 = 200 - 5 = 195$.

        39×5

        $$\begin{array}{r} 30 + 9 \\ \times \qquad 5 \\ \hline 150 + 45 \; = \; 195 \end{array}$$

   - Provide additional practice. You can use the worksheet on the previous page.

Activity 1.4b   **Multiply**

1. Illustrate multiplication by 10, 100, or 1000
   - Refer to **textbook p. 15**. Have students study this page. Students should see that each disc is multiplied by 10, 100, or 1000. So to multiply a number by 10, 100, or 1000, we can multiply the digit in each place by 10, 100, or 1000.
   - Lead students to see that the result is the same as simply adding on the correct number of 0's (1, 2, or 3) to the number.
   - Have students do **task 1, textbook p. 16**.

2. Discuss multiplication by tens, hundreds, or thousands.
   - Write a multiplication problem involving multiplication of a whole number by ones. Have students solve the problem mentally or with the multiplication algorithm.
   - Write the same problem except the ones as tens. Show students how to do the problem in two steps. Point out that to multiply by 30, we can multiply by 3, and then add one 0.

        $45 \times 3 = 135$

        45×30

        $$45 \xrightarrow{\;\times 3\;} 135 \xrightarrow{\;\times 10\;} 1350$$

   - Write the same problem using hundreds. This can also be done in two steps. This time we add two 0's.

        45×300

        $$45 \xrightarrow{\;\times 3\;} 135 \xrightarrow{\;\times 100\;} 13{,}500$$

   - Write the same problem using thousands. Now we add three 0's.

        45×3000

        $$45 \xrightarrow{\;\times 3\;} 135 \xrightarrow{\;\times 1000\;} 135{,}000$$

3. Have students do **tasks 2-4, textbook p. 16**.

Copyright © 2005 SingaporeMath.com Inc., Oregon

4. Multiply tens, hundreds, and thousands by each other.
   - Write a problem such as 300 x 20 on the board. Show students that we can solve 300 x 20 in two steps, 300 x 2 x 10. But we can also solve 300 x 2 in the same way that we would solve 2 x 300, in two steps as 2 x 3 x 100. So 300 x 20 = 2 x 3 x 100 x 10. 100 x 10 is 1000. So to multiply 300 x 20, we can simply multiply the non-zero digits together, and then add the correct number of 0's.

$$300 \times 20 = 300 \times 2 \times 10$$
$$= 2 \times 300 \times 10$$
$$= 2 \times 3 \times 100 \times 10$$
$$= 6 \times 1000$$
$$= 6000$$
$$3\underline{00} \times 2\underline{0} = 6\underline{000}$$

   - Repeat with a number such as 500 x 800 where the two non-zero digits gives a product with a 0; that is 5 x 8 = 40. We then add four 0's to the 20.

$$5000 \times 800 = 5000 \times 8 \times 100$$
$$= 8 \times 5000 \times 100$$
$$= 8 \times 5 \times 1000 \times 100$$
$$= 40 \times 100,000$$
$$= 4,000,000$$
$$5\underline{000} \times 8\underline{00} = 4,0\underline{00,000}$$

   - We can take off trailing 0's, multiply the numbers together without them, and then add the same number of 0's back onto the product.

5. Discuss estimation.
   - Write the expression 2934 x 6. Remind students that to estimate the answer to this, we round the first factor to get a number with one non-zero digit. To do this, we round it to thousands. 2934 x 6 ≈ 3000 x 6.

$$2934 \times 6 \approx 3000 \times 6$$
$$3000 \times 6 = 18,000$$

   - Write the expression 2934 x 62. Tell students that we can estimate the answer to this by rounding both factors to a number with one non-zero digit. In this example, we round 2934 to the nearest thousand, and 62 to the nearest ten.

$$2934 \times 62 \approx 3000 \times 60$$
$$3000 \times 60 = 180,000$$

   - We will see later that estimating our answer helps us check if the actual answer we get is reasonable, particularly with respect to the number of place values. (Multiplication by a 2-digit number will be reviewed in the next unit — do not require students to find actual answers at this time.)

6. Have student do **tasks 5-8, textbook p. 16**.

Workbook Exercise 5

Copyright © 2005 SingaporeMath.com Inc., Oregon

Part 5: Dividing by Tens, Hundreds or Thousands	1 session

Objectives

* Divide a whole number by 10, 100, or 1000.
* Divide a whole number by tens, hundreds, or thousands (no remainder).
* Estimate the answer in the division of a whole number by a 2-digit number.

Materials

* Number discs (discs with 1, 10, 100, 1000 and 10,000 written on them)

Homework

* Workbook Exercise 6

Notes

In *Primary Mathematics 4A*, students learned to divide a 2-digit, a 3-digit, or a 4-digit number that had 0 in the ones place by 10 by simply removing the 0. This was reviewed in Activity 1.3b. When we divide a single digit number by a number that is one or more digits with 0's following it, we can take off the trailing 0's, divide, and then add the trailing 0's back on. When we take off the trailing 0's, we look for a number that is a multiple of the number we are dividing by, so we may need to leave one of the 0's on.

$$45,000 \div 3 = 45 \text{ thousands} \div 3 = 15 \text{ thousands} = 15,000$$
$$30,000 \div 6 = 30 \text{ thousands} \div 6 = 5 \text{ thousands} = 5000$$

To divide a whole number that has 0 in the ones place by tens, we can do it in two steps:

$$45,000 \div 30$$

$$45,000 \xrightarrow{\div 10} 4500 \xrightarrow{\div 3} 1500$$

We can find $45,000 \div 30$ by removing a 0 from 45,000 and from 30, and then dividing 4500 by 3 mentally or with the division algorithm. Notice that when dividing 4500 by 3, we divide 45 by 3 and then add on the two 0's. We do not add back on any 0's that we took off of *both* numbers. So

$$\begin{aligned} 45 \text{ thousands} \div 3 \text{ tens} &= 45 \text{ thousands} \div \text{ten} \div 3 \\ &= 45 \text{ hundreds} \div 3 \\ &= 15 \text{ hundreds} \end{aligned}$$

Similarly, to divide a whole number that ends in at least two 0's by hundreds, we remove two of the zeros and then divide by the digit in the hundreds place:

$$45,0\cancel{0}\cancel{0} \div 3\cancel{0}\cancel{0} = 150$$

To divide by thousands, we first remove three zeros.

$$45,\cancel{0}\cancel{0}\cancel{0} \div 3\cancel{0}\cancel{0}\cancel{0} = 15$$

So to divide by tens, hundreds, or thousands, we take off the same number of 0's from both, and then divide the numbers.

Copyright © 2005 SingaporeMath.com Inc., Oregon

Activity 1.5a   **Divide**

1. Illustrate division by 10, 100, or 1000.
   - Refer to **textbook p. 17**. Have students study this page. Students should see that each disc represented in the number is divided by 10, 100, or 1000. Point out that when we divide each thousand or hundred by 10, we remove a zero. When we divide each thousand or hundred by 100, we remove two zeros. And when we divide by 1000, we remove three 0's.
   - Lead students to see that the results are the same as what we would get by removing the same number of zeros as the number of zeros in the number we are dividing by.
   - Have students do **task 1, textbook p. 18**.

2. Discuss division by tens, hundreds, or thousands.
   - Write the expression 45,000 ÷ 3. Have students solve the problem mentally or with the division algorithm. Remind them that we can simply take off trailing 0's until we get to a multiple of the number we are dividing by, divide, and then add back the 0's back on. 45 thousands ÷ 3 = 15 thousands.

   $45,000 \div 3 = 15$

   $$\begin{array}{r} 15,000 \\ 3\overline{)45,000} \\ \underline{3} \\ 15 \\ \underline{15} \\ 0 \end{array}$$

   - Write the expression 45,000 ÷ 30. Show students how to do the problem in two steps. To divide by 30, we can first divide by 10, then by 3. To divide by 10, we remove one 0. The end result is that we remove a 0 from both 45,000 and 30. (If students already realize that fractions can represent division, you can show the problem as a fraction and show students that we are simplifying the fraction. The relationship between division and fractions will be covered more thoroughly in unit 3.)

   $45,000 \div 30$

   $$45,000 \xrightarrow{\div 10} 4500 \xrightarrow{\div 3} 1500$$

   $$\begin{array}{r} 15\,00 \\ 3\cancel{0}\overline{)45,00\cancel{0}} \\ \underline{3} \\ 15 \\ \underline{15} \\ 0 \end{array}$$

   - Write the expression 45,000 ÷ 300. Lead students to see that this can also be done in two steps. This time we remove two 0's.

   $45,000 \div 300$

   $$45,000 \xrightarrow{\div 100} 450 \xrightarrow{\div 3} 150$$

   $$\begin{array}{r} 15\,0 \\ 3\cancel{0}\cancel{0}\overline{)45,0\cancel{0}\cancel{0}} \\ \underline{3} \\ 15 \\ \underline{15} \\ 0 \end{array}$$

   - Write the expression 45,000 ÷ 3000. Lead students to see that now we remove three 0's.

   $45,000 \div 3000$

   $$45,000 \xrightarrow{\div 1000} 45 \xrightarrow{\div 3} 15$$

   $$\begin{array}{r} 15 \\ 3\cancel{0}\cancel{0}\cancel{0}\overline{)45,\cancel{0}\cancel{0}\cancel{0}} \\ \underline{3} \\ 15 \\ \underline{15} \\ 0 \end{array}$$

3. Have students do **tasks 2-4, textbook p. 18**.

Copyright © 2005 SingaporeMath.com Inc., Oregon

4. Discuss estimation.
   • Write a problem involving division by a 1-digit number. Remind students that to estimate the answer to a problem such as 5423 ÷ 8, we rounded 5428 to the closest multiple of 8; 5600. 5423 ÷ 8 ≈ 5600 ÷ 8.

   $$5423 \div 8 \approx 5600 \div 8$$
   $$= 700$$

   • Write a problem involving division by a 2-digit number. Tell students that we can estimate the answer by rounding the number we are dividing by (the dividend) to a number with one non-zero digit. Then we round the number being divided (the divisor) to the closest multiple. In this example, we round 83 to 80, and 5423 to 5600, since 56 is a multiple of 8, and is closer to the 54 of 5423 than another multiple.

   $$5423 \div 83 \approx 5600 \div 80$$
   $$= 70$$

   • Provide some other examples.
   • We will see later that estimation will help in solving division problems where we will be dividing by a 2-digit number, and in seeing if the actual answer we get is reasonable, particularly with respect place value.

5. Have student do **tasks 5-6, textbook p. 18**.

Workbook Exercise 6

Copyright © 2005 SingaporeMath.com Inc., Oregon

Part 6: Order of Operations   **5 sessions**

Objectives

- Use mental math concepts to solve addition or multiplication problems involving more than two terms.
- Do mixed operations that involve all four operations, applying the rules for order of operation.

Materials

- Number discs (discs with 1, 10, 100, 1000 and 10,000 written on them)
- Number cards 0-9, four sets per group
- Operation cards **+**, **-**, x, and ÷, =, and parentheses cards **(** and **)**, eight sets per group

Homework

- Workbook Exercise 7
- Workbook Exercise 8

Notes

If an expression involves only addition, we can add in any order. (Addition is commutative — changing the order of addends does not change the sum — and associative — changing the grouping of addends does not change the sum.)

$$\underline{42 + 25} + 75 = 67 + 75 = 142 \quad \text{or} \quad 42 + \underline{25 + 75} = 42 + 100 = 142$$

Note that the second method is easier because there were two numbers that are easy to add mentally. When adding lists of numbers, we can look for compatible pairs of numbers, that is, numbers that they can easily add mentally. These can be numbers that make 10, 100, or that end in 5 or 0.

$$35 + 32 + 41 + 68 + 25 = 100 + 60 + 41 = 201$$

(with 35 + 25 grouped as 100 above, and 32 + 68 grouped as 60 below)

We often encounter numbers in columns, in which case it is helpful to look for pairs that make 10. Another mental technique is to add the first two numbers in a column, and if it is more than 10, just put a line under one of the numbers, and then just add the ones to the next number. Continue down the column that way, and then write the final number of ones under the column, add up all the lines indicating tens, and write the tens above the next higher place value. You may want to give students some practice adding columns of numbers. It is a good way to practice addition facts. (In the illustrations below, the 3 at the top comes from adding the ones, resulting in 36, so it is above the tens column.)

20+6

```
    3
    45
    39      20+9+7
    28
    17
    62
    75
   266
```

```
          3+4=7     45
          7+3=10    39    5+9=14
                    28    4+8=12
                    17    2+7=9
          2+1+6 = 9 62    9+2=11
          9+7= 16   75    1+5=6
   Total 2 and 6   266    3 tens 6 ones
```

Copyright © 2005 SingaporeMath.com Inc., Oregon

If an expression involves only subtraction, we subtract from left to right. Subtraction is not commutative or associative.

$$\underline{10 - 4} - 3 = 6 - 3 = 3 \qquad (\textbf{not } 10 - \underline{4 - 3} = 10 - 1 = 9)$$

Note: The numbers can be subtracted from the first number in any order, but the subtraction sign must stay with the number following it. So 10 – 4 – 3 = 10 – 3 – 4. This is not the same as doing 4 – 3 first; we are not supposed to subtract from the 4. But we can subtract 4 from 10 and then 3 from the difference, or 3 from 10 and 4 from the difference. With a problem like 115 – 20 – 15 we can do it as 115 – 15 – 20 = 100 – 20 = 80, but we can **not** subtract 15 from 20 first as in 115 – $\underline{20 - 15}$ = 115 – 5 = 110. Some students may discover this on their own, but do not teach it at this point. In the secondary level students will learn that subtraction is equivalent to adding a negative number, so if all terms being subtracted are expressed as the addition of negative numbers then it is an addition problem which is commutative and associative.

If an expression involves both addition and subtraction, we add and subtract from left to right.

$$\underline{22 - 8} + 10 = 14 + 10 = 24$$

If the expression involves only multiplication, we can multiply in any order (multiplication is commutative and associative). So we can look for factors that are easy to multiply mentally.

$$\overset{\overbrace{100}}{25 \times 36 \times 4} = 100 \times 36 = 3600$$

If the expression involves only division, we divide from left to right.

$$\underline{32 \div 4} \div 2 = 8 \div 2 = 4 \qquad (\textbf{not } 32 \div \underline{4 \div 2} = 32 \div 2 = 16)$$

If an expression involves both multiplication and division, we multiply or divide from left to right (multiplication does not have precedence over division).

$$\underline{32 \div 4} \times 2 = 8 \times 2 = 16 \qquad (\textbf{not } 32 \div \underline{4 \times 2} = 32 \div 8 = 4)$$

If an expression involves all four operations, we first do multiplication and division from left to right, and then addition and subtraction from left to right. Multiplication and division take precedence over addition and subtraction.

$$10 - \underline{4 \div 2} + 6 \times 5$$
$$= 10 - 2 + \underline{6 \times 5}$$
$$= \underline{10 - 2} + 30$$
$$= 8 + 30$$
$$= 38$$

Copyright © 2005 SingaporeMath.com Inc., Oregon

Note that 4 ÷ 2 can be done at the same time as 6 x 5 in this instance, since the result from one does not affect the result from the other. This is not the case in the following, where the first division operation must be done before the second multiplication operation:

$$10 - \underline{4 \div 2} \times 5$$
$$= 10 - \underline{2 \ \times 5}$$
$$= \underline{10 - \ \ \ \ \ 10}$$
$$= \ \ \ \ \ \ 0$$

Students may take shortcuts if they thoroughly understand the process and whether the shortcut will affect the outcome. Otherwise, require that the operations be done one step at a time, since that will lead to a correct answer.

Order of operations is taught in many elementary school texts using the mnemonic "Please Excuse My Dear Aunt Sally" for Parentheses, Exponents, Multiplication and Division, Addition and Subtraction. Other English speaking countries might use BIDMAS for Brackets, Indices, Division and Multiplication, Addition and Subtraction.

This memory device often leads to confusion later when students simply rely on the mnemonic and forget that multiplication and division are treated at the same level as are addition and subtraction. Do NOT teach your students this mnemonic. The confusion resulting from it is quite prevalent, to the extent that even occasional math internet sites show incorrect steps.

The Mental Math 2 on the next page (p. 28) is used in Activity 1.6a. Answers are given here:

Mental Math 2

1.	33	16.	280
2.	75	17.	3500
3.	250	18.	8600
4.	190	19.	330
5.	350	20.	16,000
6.	320	21.	450
7.	132	22.	7200
8.	145	23.	210
9.	199	24.	420
10.	221	25.	3600
11.	120	26.	210,000
12.	242	27.	36,000
13.	318	28.	140,000
14.	346	29.	0
15.	549	30.	3000

Copyright © 2005 SingaporeMath.com Inc., Oregon

Mental Math

1. 7 + 4 + 5 + 3 + 8 + 6 = _____

2. 30 + 25 + 20 = _____

3. 80 + 50 + 75 + 20 + 25 = _____

4. 45 + 65 + 45 + 35 = _____

5. 35 + 230 + 15 + 70 = _____

6. 130 + 50 + 20 + 70 + 50 = _____

7. 48 + 32 + 52 = _____

8. 23 + 45 + 77 = _____

9. 54 + 62 + 45 + 38 = _____

10. 32 + 34 + 68 + 21 + 66 = _____

11. 31 + 29 + 32 + 28 = _____

12. 194 + 31 + 9 + 8 = _____

13. 5 + 243 + 3 + 57 + 8 + 2 = _____

14. 164 + 25 + 36 + 46 + 75 = _____

15. 192 + 209 + 99 + 49 = _____

16. 28 x 5 x 2 = _____

17. 20 x 35 x 5 = _____

18. 86 x 25 x 4 = _____

19. 2 x 11 x 15 = _____

20. 8 x 4 x 250 x 2 = _____

21. 5 x 5 x 9 x 2 = _____

22. 9 x 50 x 2 x 8 = _____

23. 15 x 7 x 2 = _____

24. 7 x 5 x 3 x 4 = _____

25. 50 x 9 x 2 x 4 = _____

26. 500 x 7 x 2 x 30 = _____

27. 150 x 4 x 2 x 30 = _____

28. 50 x 50 x 14 x 4 = _____

29. 24 x 3 x 6 x 0 x 4 = _____

30. 125 x 3 x 8 = _____

Copyright © 2005 SingaporeMath.com Inc., Oregon

Activity 1.6a   **Mental Math**

1. Discuss addition of lists of numbers by first finding groups that can be easily added mentally.
    *   Ask students if 3 + 4 gives the same answer as 4 + 3. It does. Tell them that addition can be done in any order.
    *   Ask them if 3 + 4 + 6 is the same as 4 + 3 + 6. What about 4 + 6 + 3? Lists of numbers can also be added in any order. Ask them if one of the orders makes the addition problem easier. 4 and 6 is 10, and it is easy to add 3 to that. Looking for pairs or groups of numbers that make 10 and adding them together first makes this problem easier to do.
    *   Have students solve 8 + 3 + 2 + 7 mentally.

$$\overbrace{8 + \underbrace{3 + 2}_{10} + 7}^{10} = 20$$

    *   Write the problem 25 + 21 + 15 + 9 + 75 and ask for suggestions on how to do the problem. Lead students to see that they can try to find pairs that make 100, or add pairs that end in 0 or 5 first. You can have student find the answer by adding the numbers in the order they are written to show that this gives the same answer.

$$\overbrace{25 + \underbrace{21 + 15 + 9}_{30} + 75}^{100} = 145$$

    *   Students who have used earlier levels of *Primary Mathematics* have a lot of experience recognizing pairs of numbers that make 100. You may want to point out that to find pairs of numbers that make 100, they want to look for pairs where the sum of the ones is 10, and then see if the sum of the tens is 9. 63 and 37 are a pair that makes 100, since 3 + 7 = 10 and 60 + 30 make 9. 25 + 75 make 100, since the ones 5 + 5 = 10 and 20 + 70 = 90. Students in the U.S. may find it easy to think in quarters for this pair (25 is one quarter, 75 is 3 quarters, 4 quarters make a dollar.)
    *   You can also rewrite the problem vertically and show students how to find combinations of numbers that make 10 in each column. Some students may find it easier than finding pairs that make 100.

$$
\begin{array}{r}
2 \\
25 \\
21 \\
15 \\
9 \\
\underline{75} \\
145
\end{array}
\quad
\begin{array}{l}
20+5 \\
10+4
\end{array}
$$

    *   Provide some additional problems and have students discuss ways to find the sum.
        ➤ 15 + 20 + 25 + 35 + 30
        ➤ 85 + 65 + 35 + 15 + 75 + 25
        ➤ 59 + 73 + 27
        ➤ 92 + 28 + 8
        ➤ 153 + 349 + 51   (359 + 51 = 400)
        ➤ 179 + 152 + 21   (179 + 21 = 200)
        ➤ 96 + 97 + 98 + 99 + 100 + 101 + 102 + 103 + 104 (combine pairs to make 200)

Copyright © 2005 SingaporeMath.com Inc., Oregon

2. Discuss multiplication of lists of numbers by first finding groups that can be easily multiplied mentally.
   - Ask students if lists of numbers can be multiplied in any order. They can. Provide some examples, such as 2 x 4 = 4 x 2, 2 x 16 x 5 = 5 x 2 x 16. Point out that multiplying 5 and 2 first to get 10 makes the problem easier.
   - Have students solve 5 x 7 x 5 x 8 x 2 x 2 mentally.

$$\overset{\displaystyle 10}{\overbrace{5 \times 7 \times \underbrace{5 \times 8 \times 2}_{} \times 2}} = 5600$$
$$\underset{\displaystyle 10}{}$$

   - Have students solve 72 x 25 x 4 mentally. Point out, if necessary, that 25 x 4 = 100.

$$72 \times \overset{\displaystyle 100}{\overbrace{25 \times 4}} = 7200$$

   - Provide some additional problems and have students discuss ways to find the product.
     - 46 x 5 x 2
     - 20 x 1 x 2
     - 4 x 8 x 50   (try 4 x 50 = 200, then double 8 and add two 0's)
     - 15 x 3 x 2 x 2 x 15   (30 x 30 x 3, or 90 x 30)
     - 10 x 34 x 2 x 50
     - 5 x 3 x 12   (do 5 x 12 = 60 first)
     - 24 x 26 x 0 x 2 x 4 x 5   (0, of course)

3. (Just for fun)
   - Ask students to find the answer to 3 x 37. (111)
   - Ask them to use that information to find the answer to 6 x 37. Lead them to see that since 6 = 2 x 3, then 6 x 37 = 2 x 3 x 37 = 2 x 111 = 222.
   - Have them solve the following:
     - 12 x 37
     - 18 x 37
     - 24 x 37
     - 30 x 37

4. Use the Mental Math 2 worksheet for additional practice.

Activity 1.6b   **Order of Operations**

1. Discuss order of operations in subtraction.
   - Ask students whether it matters in what order we do subtraction. Point out that 5 from 7 is 2, but 7 from 5 is not. To help them see this clearly, draw a number line and show what happens when you take 5 from 7. Then see that 7 from 5 will lead to a point to the left of 0. Tell students that in a later grade they will learn about negative numbers, but for now they need to pay attention to the fact that the answer to 7 – 5 is different from the answer to 5 – 7.

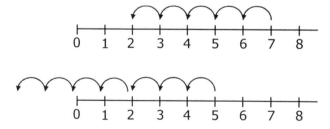

   - Because we start with a total which we take away from, subtraction cannot be done in any order. Changing the order changes the value of the total. Addition can be done in any order because we have two parts, and it does not matter which part we use first.

Copyright © 2005 SingaporeMath.com Inc., Oregon

- Write a subtraction problem involving more than two terms. Tell students that we solve subtraction problems by working from left to right.

$$
\begin{aligned}
& \underline{20 - 5} - 4 - 1 \\
= {} & \underline{15\ -4} - 1 \\
= {} & \underline{11\ \ -1} \\
= {} & 10
\end{aligned}
$$

- Show students that if we first found 5 – 4 – 1 = 0 and then subtracted that from 20 we get a different answer. To get the correct answer, we have to subtract each number from the number before it in order.

- Write a problem involving both addition and subtraction. Tell students that a problem with both addition and subtraction is also done in order from left to right. Step through the problem, underlining each operation.

$$
\begin{aligned}
& \underline{90 - 40} + 10 \\
= {} & \underline{50\ \ +10} \\
= {} & 60
\end{aligned}
$$

- Use some problems from **task 1, textbook p. 20** for additional examples. Have students do the rest of the problems in the task individually.

2. Discuss order of operation in multiplication and division.
    - Ask students whether the order matters for division problems. Write the problem 32 ÷ 4 ÷ 2 and work through the problem from left to right. Ask them if we would get the same answer if we first did 4 ÷ 2 and then divided 12 by that answer. We do not. With division, we also are starting with a total and dividing that. We do not get the same answer if we switch the number that is used as the total. Division is done from left to right in order.

$$
\begin{aligned}
& \underline{32 \div 4} \div 2 \\
= {} & \underline{8\ \ \div 2} \\
= {} & 4
\end{aligned}
$$

    - Illustrate a problem involving both multiplication and division. When we have both multiplication and division, we work it from left to right doing each operation in order. You can show that the answer will be different if we do it in a different order.

$$
\begin{aligned}
& \underline{32 \div 4} \times 2 \\
= {} & \underline{8\ \ \times 2} \\
= {} & 16
\end{aligned}
$$

- Use some problems from **task 2, textbook p. 20** for additional examples. Have students do the rest of the problems in the task individually.

Activity 1.6c   **Order of Operations without Parentheses**

1. Discuss order of operation in problems containing both multiplication/division and addition/subtraction.
    - Have students look at **textbook p. 19.**
    - Tell your student that the equation given on this page can be used to find the total number of stamps. From looking at the picture, we know that we must first multiply 4 x 3 and then add the product to 10 to get the total number of stamps.
    - If, on each of 3 pages, the boy had put 10 of one kind of stamp and 4 of a different kind, what equation should he write to show the total number of stamps? He might write the same equation: 10 + 4 x 3 = 14 x 3 = 42. The equation would give two different answers, depending on the problem it represented. So we need a way to indicate in which order the problem should be done, multiplication first or addition first.

$$
\begin{aligned}
& 10 + 4 \times 3 = 22 \\
& \text{or ?} \\
& 10 + 4 \times 3 = 42 \\[6pt]
& 10 + \underline{4 \times 3} = 10 + 12 \\
& \text{not} \\
& \underline{10 + 4} \times 3 = 14 \times 3
\end{aligned}
$$

    - By convention, when there is nothing else in the problem to tell us what order to do the operations, we do multiplication or division first, then addition or subtraction.

Copyright © 2005 SingaporeMath.com Inc., Oregon

- If we want to show that the addition should be done first, we put parenthesis around the part of the equation that should be done first: (10 + 4) x 3. The parentheses tell us that the addition should be done first.

$(10 + 4) \times 3$

- We could write parenthesis around the multiplication part to show that the multiplication should be done first, 10 + (4 x 3).

$10 + (4 \times 3)$

- But if there are no parentheses, we follow the convention of doing the multiplication first.

$10 + \underline{4 \times 3}$

- Have students read the rule in the box on p. 19. *Order of operation* simply means the order in which we compute the operations in a problem such as this.
- Tell students that if the problem has more operations, we first do all the multiplication or division from left to right, and then all the addition and subtraction. Provide some examples.

$$10 - \underline{4 \div 2} + 6 \times 5$$
$$= 10 - \quad 2 \quad + \underline{6 \times 5}$$
$$= 10 - \quad 2 \quad + 30$$
$$= \quad 8 \quad\quad + 30$$
$$= \quad\quad 38$$

2. Have students do **task 3, textbook p. 20.**

$$100 - \underline{7 \times 42} \div 3 + 18$$
$$= 100 - \quad 294 \quad \div 3 + 18$$
$$= 100 - \quad\quad 98 \quad + 18$$
$$= \quad\quad 2 \quad\quad + 18$$
$$= \quad\quad 20$$

3. Game

   Material for each group of about 4: 4 sets of number cards 0-9, about 8 sets of operation cards **+**, **-**, x, and ÷.

   Procedure: For each round shuffle the number cards and deal 6 cards to each player face up. Turn one more card face up and place in the center. Place the operation cards in the center so they are available to all players. Each player must form an expression whose answer is the number in the middle, using any of the four operations. For example, if the card in the middle is a 6, a player with the cards 3, 4, 6 and 9 can make the expression 6 x 3 ÷ 9 + 4. The player gets one point for each number card used. The first player who gets 25 points first wins.

   Workbook Exercise 7

Activity 1.6d   **Order of Operations with Parentheses**

1. Discuss order of operation in problems with parentheses.
   - Refer to **task 4, textbook p. 20**.
   - Write the problem on the board. Tell students that the parentheses tell us which operations to do first. We treat the problem in the parentheses as an expression we need to find the value for first. Once we find the value for it, we use that value in the rest of the problem.

$$27 - 2 \times \underline{(3 + 5)}$$
$$= 27 - \underline{2 \times \quad 8}$$
$$= 27 - \quad 16$$
$$= \quad 11$$

   - Tell students that if we have multiplication or division and addition or subtraction in the parenthesis, we follow the order of operation to find the value in the parenthesis. Give an example, such as the one shown here.

$$23 - (8 + \underline{2 \times 5}) \div 6$$
$$= 23 - (8 + \quad 10 \quad) \div 6$$
$$= 23 - \quad \underline{18 \quad \div 6}$$
$$= 23 - \quad\quad 3$$
$$= \quad\quad 20$$

2. Have students do **tasks 5-6, textbook p. 20.**

Copyright © 2005 SingaporeMath.com Inc., Oregon

3. Ask students to use the digit 4 four times in an expression with any of the four operations, with or without parentheses, to make up the numbers from 0 to 9. More than one solution is possible. Students can work in groups.

$$(4 + 4) - (4 + 4) = 0$$
$$(4 + 4) \div (4 + 4) = 1$$
$$4 \div 4 + 4 \div 4 = 2$$
$$(4 + 4 + 4) \div 4 = 3$$
$$4 \times (4 - 4) + 4 = 4$$
$$(4 \times 4 + 4) \div 4 = 5$$
$$(4 + 4) \div 4 + 4 = 6$$
$$4 + 4 - (4 \div 4) = 7$$
$$4 + 4 + 4 - 4 = 8$$
$$4 \div 4 + 4 + 4 = 9$$

Workbook Exercise 8

Activity 1.6e   **Practice**

1. Use **Practice 1C, textbook p. 21** to review topics covered so far.

2. Write some of the following problems and ask your student to insert parentheses if needed so that the problem's answer is the one given. Students can work in groups. They can make up their own puzzles for other students in the group to solve.

	Solution:
$2 + 4 \div 2 = 3$	$(2 + 4) \div 2$
$6 - 2 \times 3 = 0$	$6 - (2 \times 3)$
$2 \times 4 - 3 + 2 = 7$	$(2 \times 4) - 3 + 2$
$2 \times 4 - 3 + 2 = 4$	$2 \times (4 - 3) + 2$
$2 \times 4 - 3 + 2 = 3$	$2 \times 4 - (3 + 2)$
$12 - 3 \times 2 + 9 = 15$	$12 - (3 \times 2) + 9$
$12 - 3 \times 2 + 9 = 99$	$(12 - 3) \times (2 + 9)$
$24 \div 6 \div 2 + 3 = 5$	$24 \div 6 \div 2 + 3$
$24 \div 6 \div 2 + 3 = 11$	$24 \div (6 \div 2) + 3$
$2 \times 6 - 1 + 8 = 3$	$2 \times 6 - (1 + 8)$
$14 \div 1 + 6 \times 8 - 1 = 15$	$14 \div (1 + 6) \times 8 - 1$
$4 + 2 \times 7 - 9 \times 4 = 6$	$(4 + 2) \times 7 - (9 \times 4)$
$2 + 3 \times 6 - 3 \times 7 + 1 = 8$	$(2 + 3) \times 6 - (3 \times 7 + 1)$
$6 + 2 \times 9 - 13 - 7 \times 7 = 30$	$(6 + 2) \times 9 - (13 - 7) \times 7$
$8 \times 10 - 36 \div 9 + 2 - 2 \times 5 \times 5 = 0$	$8 \times (10 - 36 \div 9) + 2 - 2 \times 5 \times 5$

Game

Material for each group: 4 sets of number cards 0-9, about 8 sets of operation cards +, -, x, and ÷, =, and parenthesis cards **(** and **)**.

Procedure: For each round, shuffle the number cards and deal 6 cards to each player face up. Make the operation and parenthesis cards available to all players. Each player must form an equation with his cards. The player gets one point for each number card used. The player who gets 25 points first wins. For example, a player with the cards 2, 4, 4, 6, 7 and 9 can make the equations

$$(4 + 2) \times 7 - 9 \times 4 = 6 \qquad \text{or} \qquad (4 + 4) \div 2 + (9 - 6) = 7$$

Copyright © 2005 SingaporeMath.com Inc., Oregon

| **Part 7: Word Problems** | **4 sessions** |

Objectives

* Solve multi-step word problems

Homework

* Workbook Exercise 9
* Workbook Exercise 10

Notes

In *Primary Mathematics 3*, students learned to draw part-whole and comparison models to illustrate concepts and to solve 1-step and 2-step word problems. In this section they will be solving word problems of 2-steps or more.

Part-whole model for addition and subtraction

The total is made up of two or more parts.

If the problem gives the parts, we use the model to see that we add to find the whole. For example:

There are 20 marbles in a bag. Sam put in 10 more marbles. How many are in the bag now?

$$20 + 10 = 30$$

There are 30 marbles total.

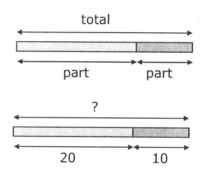

If the problem gives a part and the total, we can see from the model that we subtract to find the missing part. For example:

There are 30 red and blue marbles in a bag. 20 were red marbles. How many blue marbles are there?

$$30 - 20 = 10$$

There are 10 blue marbles.

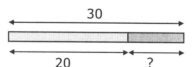

Comparison model for addition and subtraction

Two (or more) quantities are compared. We draw two bars, one longer than the other, to represent the two quantities.

If the problem gives the value of one quantity and the difference between the two quantities, we can see from the model that we can find the value of the other quantity by addition. For example:

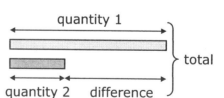

Copyright © 2005 SingaporeMath.com Inc., Oregon

A bag has red and blue marbles. There are 80 blue marbles. There are 120 more red marbles than blue marbles. How many marbles are there?

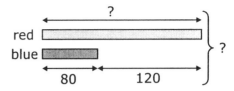

Number of red marbles = 80 + 120 = 200
Total number of marbles = 200 + 80 = 280

If the problem gives the value of both quantities, we can find the difference by subtraction. Or, if the problem gives the value of the larger number and the difference, we can see from the model that we can find the value of the second quantity by subtraction. For example:

There are red and blue marbles in a bag. There are 200 red marbles. There are 120 more red marbles than blue marbles. How many marbles are in the bag?

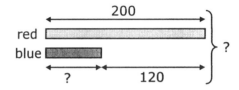

Number of blue marbles = 200 – 120 = 80
Total number of marbles = 200 + 80 = 280

If the problem gives the total and the difference between the quantities, we can find the value of the smaller quantity by subtracting the difference from the total and dividing the result by 2. For example:

There are 280 red and blue marbles in the bag. There are 120 more red marbles than blue marbles. How many blue marbles are there?

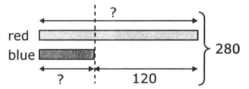

Number of blue marbles = (280 – 120) ÷ 2 = 80

Part-whole model for multiplication and division

The total is represented with a long bar which can be divided up into equal parts. Each equal part is called a **unit**.

If the problem gives the number of equal parts and the number in each part, we divide the total bar into the number of equal parts (units) and label a part with the number in the part, the value of the part. We can see from the model that we must multiply to find the total. For example:

There are 4 jars. Each has 10 marbles. Find the total number of marbles.

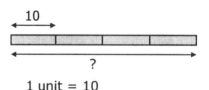

1 unit is the number of marbles in one jar.

    1 unit = 10 marbles.

The total number of marbles is 4 units.

    4 units = 10 x 4 = 40 marbles

1 unit = 10
4 units = 10 x 4 = 40

There are 40 marbles total.

Copyright © 2005 SingaporeMath.com Inc., Oregon

If the problem gives a total and the number of equal groups, divide the total bar into the number of equal parts (units) and label the total. We can see from the model that we must divide to find the amount in each unit. For example:

40 marbles are divided equally into 4 jars. Find the number of marbles in each jar.

1 unit is the number of marbles in a jar.

There are 4 units total.

    4 units = 40

We need to find the number of marbles in 1 unit.

    1 unit = 40 ÷ 4 = 10

Each jar gets 10 marbles.

4 units = 40
1 unit = 40 ÷ 4 = 10

If the problem gives the amount in each group or part, we can divide to find the number of parts. For example:

There are 40 marbles total. 10 are put into each jar. How many jars do we need? In this problem we don't know the number of units, but we know the amount in each unit. We can find the number of units by division.

    40 ÷ 10 = 4

There are 4 jars.

Comparison model for multiplication and division

In the **comparison model** for multiplication and division, two (or more) quantities are compared. We are told how many times as much one quantity is than the other. The smaller quantity is the unit. We can draw both quantities as a number of equal sized units. We generally want to find the value of one unit.

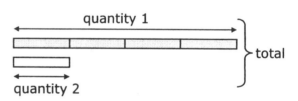

If the problem gives the smaller quantity, the amount in one unit, we can use that information to find the value of the larger quantity, the difference between the quantities, or the total amount by multiplication. For example:

There are 4 times as many blue marbles in a jar as red marbles. There are 10 red marbles. How many blue marbles are there? How many more blue marbles are there than red marbles? How many marbles are there altogether?

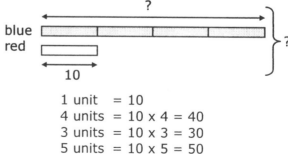

1 unit is the number of red marbles. There are 4 units of blue marbles, 3 units more blue marbles than red marbles, and 5 units of marbles altogether. From 1 unit = 10, we can find the value of 4 units, 3 units, or 5 units. There are 40 blue marbles, 30 more blue marbles than red marbles, and 50 marbles altogether.

1 unit = 10
4 units = 10 x 4 = 40
3 units = 10 x 3 = 30
5 units = 10 x 5 = 50

Copyright © 2005 SingaporeMath.com Inc., Oregon

If the problem gives the larger quantity (more than one unit), we see from the model that we can find the smaller quantity, or one unit, by division. Once we find the value for 1 unit, we can answer other questions. For example:

There are 4 times as many blue marbles in a jar as red marbles. There are 40 blue marbles.
1 unit is the number of red marbles.
Once we find the value of 1 unit (the number of red marbles) we can find the difference between the blue and red marbles and the number of total marbles.

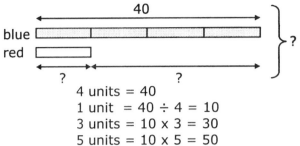

4 units = 40
1 unit = 40 ÷ 4 = 10
3 units = 10 x 3 = 30
5 units = 10 x 5 = 50

Combined models

Students have already encountered problems that can be modeled using a part-whole model where one part is a multiple of a unit. From the model, we can see which operation needs to be used to find the answer to each step of the problem.

If the problem gives one part as a multiple of a given unit, we can find the total by first finding that part by multiplication, then adding the other part. For example:

There are 4 small jars each with 10 marbles, and a large jar with 15 marbles. How many marbles are there in all?

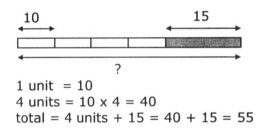

Here we have two parts, the small jars and the large jar. We can model the problem by making two parts, dividing one part into 4 units, labeling the amount in 1 unit and the amount in the other part. This helps to show that we have to first find the number of blue marbles by multiplication.

1 unit = 10
4 units = 10 x 4 = 40
total = 4 units + 15 = 40 + 15 = 55

Students have also encountered problems where a total and the differences between two or more quantities is given. To solve these types of problems, we need to get a number of equal units. For example:

There are 56 marbles in all. There are three times as many red marbles as blue marbles. There are 6 fewer blue marbles than green marbles. How many green marbles are there?

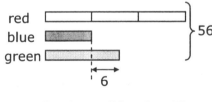

To solve this problem, we need to find the value of 1 unit. First, we need to find what a number of units are equal to so we can divide. We can see by the model that if we take away 6 green marbles, we get 5 equal units. So we can take away 6 from the total to get the value of 5 units. Then we can find the number of green marbles.

5 units = 56 – 6 = 50
1 unit = 50 ÷ 5 = 10

Modeling is a tool that can be used in solving word problems. It is not the only tool and not all problems lend themselves to modeling using bars. However, for those that do, modeling provides students with systematic means of organizing the information and determining the calculations needed to solve the problem. Some students can work out solutions to the problems in the workbook and practices by forming a mental picture of a model or without a pictorial model. Students should be able to draw a pictorial representation when necessary.

Copyright © 2005 SingaporeMath.com Inc., Oregon

Activity 1.7a   **Review of model drawing**

1. Review word problems from earlier levels. If your students have all done earlier levels of Primary Mathematics, this review may not be necessary, or may be abbreviated. For additional problems, you can use examples from the notes in the previous few pages of this guide, or refer to earlier levels of Primary Mathematics, in particular:
   ➤ *Primary Mathematics 3A*, pp. 20-23, pp. 36-38, pp. 44-48
   ➤ *Primary Mathematics 3B*, pp. 34-38
   ➤ *Primary Mathematics 4A*, pp. 33-35
   ➤ *Primary Mathematics 4B*: pp. 41-44

   • Give students a problem requiring a part-whole model for addition or subtraction. For example:

   Paul gave $134 to John and had $56 left. How much money did Paul have at first?

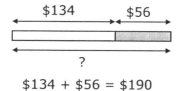

   $134 + $56 = $190

   Lead students to see that the problem gives us two parts, the money Paul gave to John and the money he has left. We can draw these two parts with bars and label them. The problem asks for the total amount of money Paul had at first. We can label that with a question mark. We see from the drawing that in order to find the answer, we need to add.

   Paul had $190 at first.

   • Give students a problem requiring comparison model for addition or subtraction. For example:

   Mary had 120 more beads than Jill. Jill had 68 beads. How many beads did the two girls have altogether?

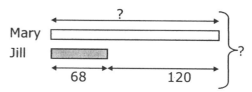

   Lead students to see that we are comparing two quantities, so we can draw them as two bars, one on top of each other, aligned at the left. Ask which bar we would draw longer. We know that Mary had more beads, so we draw her bar longer. Guide students in labeling the drawing with information from the problem.

   Step 1:
   68 + 120 = 188
   Mary had 188 beads.
   Step 2:
   188 + 68 = 256
   Together, they had 256 beads.

   Or:
   (2 x 68) + 120 = 256

   The problem asks for the total amount of beads. Ask students what we would need to add to find the total amount. We know how many beads Jill has, but we need to find how many beads Mary has. We can see from the problem that in order to find out how many beads Mary had, we need to add. After we find the number of beads Mary has, we can find the total beads.

   We could also see from the drawing that we could write one equation for the problem: (2 x 68) + 120.

Copyright © 2005 SingaporeMath.com Inc., Oregon

• Give students a problem requiring a comparison model for multiplication or division (problems which involve only a part-whole model are usually easy to solve without drawing a model). For example:

Sam bought some shoes which cost $15. He also bought some boots which cost three times as much as the shoes. How much did he spend?

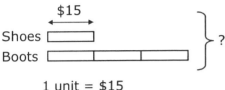

1 unit = $15
4 units total
4 units = $15 x 4 = $60
He spent $60 altogether.

Or

3 units = $15 x 3 = $45
The boots cost $45
$15 + $45 = $60
He spent $60 altogether

Tell students that here we are comparing two quantities, so we can draw one bar for the cost of the shoes and one for the cost of the boots. Ask students how they would represent the cost of the boots. Since the boots cost 3 times as much, we draw it about three times as long. We show that it is 3 times as long by drawing equal units. The cost of the shoes is 1 unit, and the cost of the boots is 3 units. Guide students in labeling the drawing. Remind them that we are finding the total. Have them suggest equations based on the drawing which will give the total. Students can see that there are 4 units total, so we can multiply 1 unit by 4. Or, we can find the cost of the boots first by multiplying one unit by 3, then adding to find the total cost.

• Discuss some additional problem involving a combination of models.

○ Mary bought 3 shirts. Each shirt cost the same amount. She gave the cashier $20 and got $2 change. How much did each dress cost?

The total is $20. One part is the change, and the other the cost of the shirts. We want to find the cost of 1 shirt. We need to find the cost of all the shirts first.
Cost of the dresses = $20 – $2 = $18
Once we find the cost of all the shirts, we can label that.
Cost of 1 dress = $18 ÷ 3 = $6

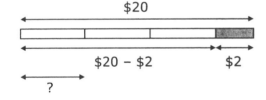

○ Peter has $12. He has twice as much money as Paul. John has $2 less than Paul. How much money does John have?

If John has $2 less than Paul, we need to find out how much money Paul has. We can find that by division.
Paul's money = 1 unit
Peter's money = 2 units
2 units = $12
1 unit = $12 ÷ 2 = $6
John's money = Paul's money – $2 = $6 – $2 = $4

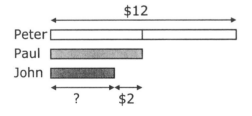

Copyright © 2005 SingaporeMath.com Inc., Oregon

Activity 1.7b   **Word problems**

1. Discuss the problem on **p. 22 of the textbook**.
   - Guide the students in relating the information in the problem to the drawing. Since this is a problem involving equal parts, we can use a part-whole model and show a unit for a bag.
   - Ask students what we need to know to find how much money she made (her profit). First, we will need to know how much money she got when she sold mangoes. What else do we need to know to find out how much her profit was? The cost of each bag [packet] and the number of bags [packets]. We know how much a bag costs.
   - We need to find how many bags she sold. The total number of bags would be the total number of units in the drawing. We can see from the drawing that to find the total number of bags, we divide 420 by 4. We now have the number of bags and can solve the problem.
   - Note that not every bit of information in the problem is modeled. We could draw an additional comparison model showing the selling price and cost price, but by now most students don't need to draw a model for this part. Some might not even have to draw a model to find the number of bags.
   - She made $252.

2. Discuss **task 1, textbook p. 23**.
   - The problem gives us information comparing two quantities, how much more Ryan received than Juan. (In the 3rd edition Raju and Samy are Ryan and Juan respectively. If you are using the 3rd edition, substitute Raju for Ryan and Samy for Juan in the discussion below.) So we can draw a comparison model for the amount each boy received.
   - Whose bar is longer? (Ryan's since he got $100 more.) Ryan's bar is drawn longer than Juan's bar, and the difference is labeled.
   - What other information do we have? (The total amount) We can label that on the diagram.
   - What do we have to find? (How much Juan received, which is the value of the shorter bar) How is that labeled on the diagram? (With a question mark.)
   - How can we find that value? We can look at the picture and see that if we take $100 off of Ryan's bar, we get the same amount for both, or two equal units. If we know what 2 units are, we can find 1 unit, which is how much Juan received.
   - Juan received $155.

3. Discuss **task 2, textbook p. 23**.
   - [Users of the 3rd edition please substitute Singapore stamps for U.S. stamps in the following discussion.] The statement that there are four times as many U.S. stamps tells us that two quantities are being compared, and that one is a multiple of the other. So we use the comparison model for multiplication and division, and show the number of U.S. stamps as 4 units and the number of foreign stamps as one unit.
   - What information are we given? (The total number of stamps) That is labeled on the diagram. What do we need to find? (The number of U.S. stamps.) How many units is this? (4)
   - If we can find one unit, we can then find 4 units. How do we find one unit? We see that 5 units equal 1170. So we can divide to find 1 unit.
   - He has collected 936 U.S. stamps.

Copyright © 2005 SingaporeMath.com Inc., Oregon

4. Discuss some additional word problems where it is helpful to model the problem, such as the following.

- Amy has 34 stickers and Sara has 20. Amy gives Sara some stickers so they both have the same number of stickers. How many stickers does Amy have now? How many stickers did Amy give to Sara?
The total number of stickers does not change. Amy ends up with 1 unit, and Sara ends up with 1 unit.
2 units = total = 34 + 20 = 54
1 unit = 54 ÷ 2 = 27
Amy now has 27 stickers.
Amount she gave to Sara = 34 – 27 = 7
Or:
Amy has 34 – 20 = 14 stickers more than
Sara. If she gives half of this, or 7, to Sara,
they will have the same number, 27 stickers.

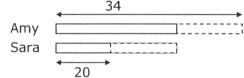

- John and Matt earn the same amount of money. If John spends $130 and Matt spends $480, John will have three times as much money left as Matt. How much money does each boy earn?

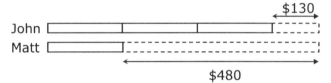

2 unit = $480 – $130 = $350
1 unit = $350 ÷ 2 = $175
Amount each boy earns
= $175 + $480 = $655

Workbook Exercise 9

Activity 1.7c   **More word problems**

1. Discuss **task 3, textbook p. 24**.
   - A part-whole model can be used here, as shown in the diagram in the text, since we are given the cost of each item, plus the total. Since two of the items are the same, we show that by drawing two of the parts the same. We could also draw an additional part to the diagram in the textbook which includes the change, and make the total $50.
   - From the diagram, we can see that since the two T-shirts cost the same, if we can find the cost of the two T-shirts, then we can find the cost of 1 T-shirt. So we can first find the amount spent, then the amount of the 2 T-shirts.
   - We could also combine this step as ($50 – $3 – $29) ÷ 2 = $9
   - The cost of each T-shirt was $9.

2. Discuss **task 4, textbook p. 24**.
   - Two quantities are being compared, with one twice as much as the other so we can use a comparison model, showing the CD to be twice the cost of a tape. From the diagram, we see that we can find the cost of one tape.

Copyright © 2005 SingaporeMath.com Inc., Oregon

- Show students an alternate model. Since the CD cost twice as much as the videotape, we can show the video tape as 1 unit and the CD as two units. But since he bought three videotapes, we can draw 3 units for the videotapes. The total amount spent is 5 units.

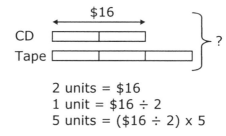

2 units = $16
1 unit = $16 ÷ 2
5 units = ($16 ÷ 2) x 5

- Point out to students that there is often more than one way to solve word problems, and there is no formula or specific procedure to follow. Many of the problems they will encounter will involve equal units. Once they can find the value of one unit, they can usually solve the problem. Finding the value of a unit involves relating the given information to each other so that we can form an equation that will give us the value of one or more units. If we can find the value of several equal units, then we can divide to find the value of one unit, and use that value to solve the problem being asked.

3. Provide some additional problem for class discussion or to allow students to work on individually or in groups and then present their solutions. You can use some of the problems in **Practice 1D, textbook p. 25**. See the next activity for possible solutions. Problems #3, #5, and #10 are particularly challenging and therefore good for discussion. The problems in workbook exercise 10 are also good for discussion. You may want to discuss the following problem:

- Five years ago, Mrs. Smith was three times as old as her daughter Mary. Now, their total age is now 42 years. How old is Mary now?

The problem involves a comparison, so we can draw 1 bar for Mary and one for her mother. If we use both Mrs. Smith's and Mary's ages as they were 5 years ago, we have one unit for Mary and 3 for Mrs. Smith. Then we add another part for the 5 years to show their current ages. We don't really know if 5 years is longer or shorter than the units, but we can draw it either way. Now we can see if we can find the value of one or more equal units. Since we have the total age, we can take 5 years off the total age for each of them and get the sum of their ages 5 years ago, which would be 4 units. From that we can find the value of 1 unit, and then Mary's current age.

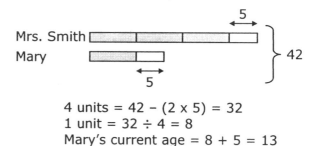

4 units = 42 – (2 x 5) = 32
1 unit = 32 ÷ 4 = 8
Mary's current age = 8 + 5 = 13

Workbook Exercise 10

Activity 1.7d   **Practice**

1. Have students work individually or in groups on the problems in **Practice D, textbook p. 25**. Then have them share their solutions. Discuss any alternate solutions. Possible solutions and explanations are given here.

Copyright © 2005 SingaporeMath.com Inc., Oregon

1. John's weight is being compared to Peter's weight, so we can try a comparison model. Since we are trying to find John's weight, we can make his weight the unit.

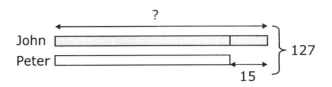

   If 15 kg is added to Peter's weight, they would both weigh the same. Add 15 to the total weight to get the total weight if both weighed the same.

   1 unit = John's weight.
   2 units = 127 kg + 15 kg = 142 kg
   1 unit = 142 ÷ 2 = 71 kg

   Or, we can make Peter's weight the unit, and get 2 units by subtracting 15 from John's weight.

   1 unit = Peter's weight
   2 units = 127 kg – 15 kg = 112 kg
   1 unit = 112 ÷ 2 = 56 kg
   John's weight = 1 unit + 15 kg
             = 56 kg + 15 kg
             = 71 kg

   John weighs 71 kg

2. There are 2 more units of boys than girls.
   2 units = 24
   1 unit = 24 ÷ 2 = 12
   4 units = 12 x 4 = 48
   There are **48** children altogether.

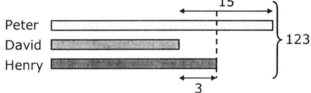

3. Three weights are being compared. Since Peter is heavier than David his bar will be longer than David's, and since David is lighter than Henry, Henry's bar is longer than David's. Since Henry is 3 kg heavier, whereas Peter is 15 kg heavier, Henry's bar will be shorter than Peter's.

   Now try to get equal units. Since the problem asks for Henry's weight, we can make that the unit.

   If 3 kg were added to David's weight, his weight would be 1 unit.

   If 15 kg – 3 kg = 12 kg is taken off Peter's weight, it would be 1 unit.

   It is not necessary to make the value being found the unit. Some students might find it simpler to make David's weight 1 unit. Discuss both methods.

   1 unit = Henry's weight.
   3 units = 123 + 3 – 12 = 114 kg
   1 unit = 114 ÷ 3 = 38 kg

   Henry weighs 38 kg.

   Or,
   1 unit = David's weight
   3 units = 123 – 15 – 3 = 105
   1 unit = 105 ÷ 3 = 35
   Henry's weight = 35 + 3 = 38 kg

4. Draw bars to show the comparison. [3rd edition: Pablo and Ryan are Ahmed and Raju respectively.]
   For them to both have an equal amount of money, Pablo would have to give Ryan half of his extra money. That is, Pablo gives Ryan half the difference. ($180 – $150) ÷ 2 = $15.
   He will have to give $15.

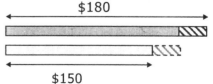

Copyright © 2005 SingaporeMath.com Inc., Oregon

5. Draw a comparison model. [3d edition: Matthew is Minghua.] Matthew has 2 units and David has 1 unit. The total does not change. In order for them to have the same amount, Matthew must give David half the difference, which is half of a unit. We can divide all the units into half so that Matthew has 4 units and David has 2. Then if Matthew gives David 1 unit, they will both have 3 units.

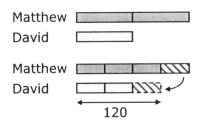

3 units = 120 stickers
1 unit = 120 ÷ 3 = 40
He must give David 40 stickers

6. [3ʳᵈ edition: Joe and Emily are Ali and Lihua.]
1 unit = 340 ÷ 4 = 85
2 units = 85 x 2 = 170
Peter has 170 stickers.

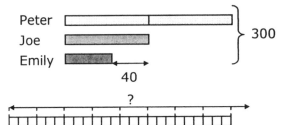

7. 3 books = 1 unit
24 books = 8 units
1 unit = $5
8 units = $5 x 8 = $40
Total money = $40 + $2 = $42
He had $42 at first.

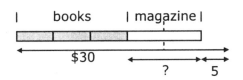

8. 1 book = 1 unit
1 magazine = 2 units
3 books + 1 magazine = 5 units
Amount he spent $30 – $5 = $25
5 units = $25
1 unit = $25 ÷ 5 = $5
2 units = $5 x 2 = $10
The magazine cost $10

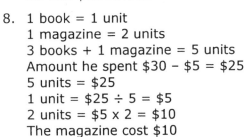

9. Remaining oranges = 155 – 15 = 140
140 ÷ 7 = 20 groups of 7 oranges
$2 x 20 = $40
His profit is $40 – $35 = $5

Or: 7 oranges for $2

1 orange for $\frac{2}{7}$

140 oranges for $\frac{2}{7}$ x 140 = $40

His profit is $40 – $35 = $5

10. Draw a bar to show the total for John and Paul, and another to show the total for John and Henry. For each, the bar for John is the same. Draw Henry's bar to show it as 3 times Paul's bar. If Paul's bar is 1 unit, we can see that John + Henry is 2 units longer than John + Paul. So we can find the value for 2 units, and then for 1 unit, which is how much Paul spent.

2 units = $65 – $45 = $20
1 unit = $20 ÷ 2 = $10
Amount John spent = $45 – $10 = $35

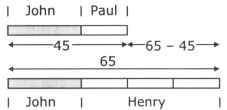

Copyright © 2005 SingaporeMath.com Inc., Oregon

Unit 2 – Multiplication and Division by a 2-digit Whole Number

Objectives

- Multiply a number of up to 4-digits by a 2-digit number.
- Divide a number of up to 4-digits by a 2-digit number.

Suggested number of sessions: 8

	Objectives	Textbook	Workbook	Activities
Part 1 : Multiplication				**2 sessions**
20	• Multiply a whole number by tens.	p. 26 p. 27, tasks 1-2	Ex. 11, #1	2.1a
	• Multiply a 2-digit or 3-digit number by a 2-digit number.	p. 27, tasks 3-4		
21	• Multiply a 4-digit number by a 2-digit number.	p. 27, tasks 5-6	Ex. 11, #2	2.1b
Part 2 : Division				**6 sessions**
	Objectives	**Textbook**	**Workbook**	
22	• Divide a whole number by tens.	p. 28 pp. 29, tasks 1-2	Ex. 12, #1	2.2a
	• Divide a 2-digit or 3-digit number by a 2-digit number where the quotient is 1 digit.	p. 29, tasks 3-5		
23	• Divide a 2-digit or 3-digit number by a 2-digit number where the quotient is 1 digit.	pp. 29-30, tasks 6-11	Ex. 12, #2	2.2b
24	• Divide a 3-digit number by a 2-digit number where the quotient is 2 digits.	p. 31, tasks 12-14	Ex 13, #1	2.2c
25	• Divide a 4-digit number by a 2-digit number.	p. 31, tasks 15-16	Ex. 13, #2	2.2d
26	• Practice. • Solve word problems involving multiplication or division by a 2-digit number.	p. 32, Practice 2A		2.2e
27	• Review • Review factors and multiples.		Review 1	2.2f

Part 1: Multiplication	**2 sessions**

Objectives

* Multiply a number of up to 4-digits by a 2-digit number.

Materials

* Number cards 0-9, 4 sets for each group of students

Homework

* Workbook Exercise 11

Notes

Students learned to multiply 2-digit and 3-digit whole numbers by a 2-digit whole number in *Primary Mathematics 4A*. This is reviewed here and extended to multiplying a 4-digit whole number by a 2-digit whole number.

Students should already be familiar with multiplying a whole number by a single digit. If not, you will have to spend at least one extra session teaching this. See Activity 2.1a in the *Primary Mathematics 4A Teacher's Guide* and Unit 2, Part 2 of *Primary Mathematics 4A*.

When we multiply a number by tens, the answer will be in tens. Thus there is a 0 in the ones place, and the product of the given number times the digit in the tens place goes to the left of this 0. For example, in 1234 x 50, we write a 0 in the ones place, and then find 1234 x 5 = 6170 (1234 x 50 = 1234 x 5 x 10).

$$\begin{array}{r} 1\,2\,3\,4 \\ \underline{\times\quad 5\mathbf{0}} \\ 6\,1\,7\,0\mathbf{0} \end{array}$$

When we multiply a whole number by a 2-digit number, we first multiply by the ones, then by the tens, and then add the two products. For example, in 1234 x 56 we first find 1234 x 6, then 1234 x 50, and then add.

$$\begin{array}{r} 1\,2\,3\,4 \\ \underline{\times\quad 5\mathbf{6}} \\ 7\,4\,0\,4 \quad\leftarrow 1234 \times 6 \\ \underline{6\,1\,7\,0\,0} \quad\leftarrow 1234 \times 50 \\ 6\,9\,1\,0\,4 \end{array}$$

Students should determine whether their answer is reasonable using estimation. For example, 1234 x 56 ≈ **1**000 x 6**0** = 6**0,000**, so 69,104 is a reasonable answer. However if a student were to forget to write the 0 down when multiplying by ten, his answer would be 13,574, which the estimate shows as an unreasonable answer. If you find students getting incorrect answers, it may help to have them estimate in steps, so that you can pinpoint the source of the error which may relate to place value, poor knowledge of the times table, or both.

Copyright © 2005 SingaporeMath.com Inc., Oregon

Activity 2.1a   **Multiply 2-digit and 3-digit numbers**

1. Review multiplying a whole number by tens.
    *   Refer to **(a) on p. 26 of the textbook**.
        o   Point out to students that Method 1 reminds us that we can multiply by tens by multiplying by the digit in the tens place and then adding a 0. Method 2 shows this in the vertical format.
        o   Guide your students through actually doing the problem, using the multiplication algorithm and paying careful attention to the place value of the digits. In 78 x 3, we first multiply 8 x 3, getting 24. (We can write a little 2 over the 7 to remind ourselves that we need to add the tens in after multiplying 70 x 3.) In 78 x 30, we first write down a 0 in the answer to help us place the digits correctly, and then multiply 78 x 3 in the same way as before. (In this case, the little 2 we write above 7 is actually 200, not a 20, even though we write it above the tens column. So is the 21 that we add it to. Writing it above the 7 is simply to remind us to add it after multiplying the 7 and 3.)

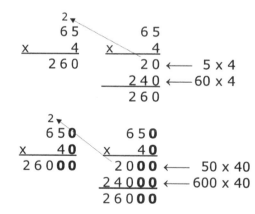

    *   Refer to **(b) on p. 26 of the textbook**.
        o   As we saw earlier, we can solve this problem by finding 65 x 4, then adding two 0's since we are multiplying 64 tens by 4 tens; and 10 x 10 = 100. 650 x 40 = 65 x 10 x 4 x 10 = 65 x 4 x 100.
        o   Again, step through 65 x 4 and then 650 x 40, paying attention to the place values.
        o   In 65 x 4, we can first multiply 5 x 4 to get 20. We write the 2 tens above the 6 to remind us to add it in after we multiply 60 x 4.
        o   In 650 x 40, we can write down two 0's, and then find 65 x 4. The 2 resulting from 5 x 4 is actually 2 thousands (50 x 40 = 2000). We still write it above the 6, even though it actually belongs one place over, so that we will remember to add it when multiplying 4 and 6 (for 40 x 600).
        o   Tell students they should always find an estimate to see if their answer is reasonable, particularly with respect to place value. 650 x 40 ≈ 600 x 40 = 24,000

2. Have students do **tasks 1-2, textbook p. 27**.
    *   You can call on some students to show their work on the board.
    *   Require students to find an estimate to check if their answers are reasonable.

Copyright © 2005 SingaporeMath.com Inc., Oregon

3. Review multiplying 2-digit and 3-digit whole numbers by a 2-digit number.
   • Refer to **task 3, textbook p. 27**.
   • Remind students that to multiply by a 2-digit number, we first multiply by the ones, and then by the tens of the 2-digit number, writing both products below the line. Then we add them.
   • Step through the problems in task 3 with your students. 3.(d) is shown here. Emphasize the place values. For example, in the last multiplication step for (d), say, "7 tens times 6 hundreds is 42 thousands. Add the thousands from regrouping…."
   • Have students find an estimate to check if their answers are reasonable.

4. Have students do **task 4, textbook p. 27**.
   • You can call on some students to show their work on the board.
   • Have students find an estimate to check if their answers are reasonable.

5. Provide additional practice.
   • You can have students work in groups. Give each group 4 sets of number cards 0-9. One student shuffles the deck. Each student draws 5 cards and makes a 3-digit and a 2-digit number with them and then multiplies these.

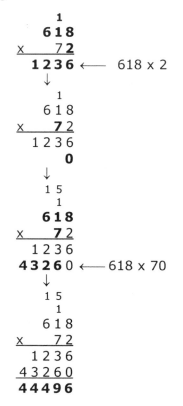

Workbook Exercise 11, #1

Copyright © 2005 SingaporeMath.com Inc., Oregon

Activity 2.1b   **Multiply 4-digit numbers**

1. Discuss multiplying a 4-digit whole number by a 2-digit number.
   - Refer to **task 5, textbook p. 27**.
   - We follow the same process with a 4-digit whole number as with a 2-digit whole number. We first multiply by the ones, and then by the tens of the 2-digit number, writing both products below the line. Then we add them.
   - Step through the problems in task 5 with your students. 5.(a) is shown here. Emphasize the place values for each step.
   - Have students find an estimate to check if their answers are reasonable.

2. Have students do **task 6, textbook p. 27**.
   - Have students find an estimate to check if their answers are reasonable.

3. Provide additional problem for practice.
   - You can give students a few problems involving multiplication by a 3-digit whole number. By now, students should be able to extend multiplication to any number of digits, and the process becomes a rather tedious mechanical one where they need to keep track of place value and be careful with their multiplication and addition facts.
   - As you move on to other topics, continue to give students several problems every once in a while, perhaps at the beginning of class, so that they can keep their skills sharp.

Workbook Exercise 11, #2

$$
\begin{array}{r}
\scriptstyle 3\ 2\ 3 \\
4\,6\,3\,5 \\
\times\quad 2\,6 \\
\hline
2\,7\,8\,1\,0 \\
\downarrow
\end{array}
$$

$$
\begin{array}{r}
\scriptstyle 3\ 2\ 3 \\
4\,6\,3\,5 \\
\times\quad 2\,6 \\
\hline
2\,7\,8\,1\,0 \\
0 \\
\downarrow
\end{array}
$$

$$
\begin{array}{r}
\scriptstyle 1\quad 1 \\
\scriptstyle 3\ 2\ 3 \\
4\,6\,3\,5 \\
\times\quad 2\,6 \\
\hline
2\,7\,8\,1\,0 \\
9\,2\,7\,0\,0 \\
\downarrow
\end{array}
$$

$$
\begin{array}{r}
\scriptstyle 1\quad 1 \\
\scriptstyle 3\ 2\ 3 \\
4\,6\,3\,5 \\
\times\quad 2\,6 \\
\scriptstyle 1\ 1 \\
2\,7\,8\,1\,0 \\
9\,2\,7\,0\,0 \\
\hline
1\,2\,0\,5\,1\,0
\end{array}
$$

Copyright © 2005 SingaporeMath.com Inc., Oregon

Part 2: Division	5 sessions

Objectives

- Divide a number of up to 4-digits by a 2-digit number.

Materials

- Number cards 0-9, 4 sets for each group of students

Homework

- Workbook Exercise 12
- Workbook Exercise 13

Notes

Students learned in earlier levels of *Primary Mathematics* how to divide a whole number by a 1-digit number. See Activity 2.1b in the *Primary Mathematics 4A Teacher's Guide* and Unit 2, Part 2 of *Primary Mathematics 4A*. Here students will learn to divide by a 2-digit number.

Students have learned the terms *quotient* and *remainder*. The terms *dividend* and *divisor* have not been formally taught in the *Primary Mathematics* yet. By now, you should help students memorize the term divisor, since it will be used regularly in later courses. Dividend is not used as much. If they know the terms quotient and divisor, if they do encounter the term dividend, they will be able to figure out that is the total.

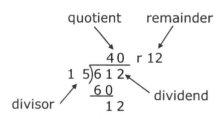

In this section we will deal only with whole number quotients. When the division is not exact, the remainder is written as a whole number, not as a fraction or a decimal.

Estimation is perhaps the central component of division. To divide any number by a 2-digit number, we use estimation to look for that multiple of the divisor which gives the value closest to the dividend. We then use that multiple to multiply the divisor, and it is this product which lets us find the remainder. When dividing a 4-digit number by a 2-digit number, we do it in steps, first finding the quotient for the thousands, if there is one, then the hundreds (including the remainder from dividing the thousands) , then the tens (including the remainder from dividing the hundreds), and then the ones (including the remainder from dividing the tens).

For example, in 9514 ÷ 64, we cannot divide the 9 (in nine thousands) by 64 so we rename thousands as hundreds. This division problem then starts with 95 hundreds divided by 64. First we estimate, rounding 64 to 60 to *estimate* 95 hundreds ÷ 60: 60 x 1 = 60, but 60 x 2 = 120 (too high). So, we will use the 1 hundred quotient.

```
        148  r 42
6 4)9 5 1 4
     6 4
     3 1 1
     2 5 6
       5 5 4
       5 1 2
         4 2
```

1 hundred x 64 hundreds = 64 hundreds. Subtract this product from 95 hundreds to get the remainder of 31 hundreds.

Copyright © 2005 SingaporeMath.com Inc., Oregon

Now we rename that remainder as tens. 31 hundreds and 1 ten is 311 tens. *Estimate* 311 ÷ 60: 60 x 5 = 300. Try 5 tens as the quotient. 5 tens x 64 = 320 tens, which is more than the remainder tens. So 5 tens is too high. Try one less ten: 4 tens x 64 = 256 tens. Subtract this product from the tens to get the remainder, 55 tens. Now we rename that remainder as ones and divide the ones.

55 tens + 4 = 554 ones. *Estimate* 554 ÷ 60. 60 x 9 = 540. Since 9 will be too high, try 8; 8 x 64 = 512. Subtract that from the ones to get the remainder, 42.

In this section, students will first divide a 2-digit or 3-digit number by tens, and then by a 2-digit number where the quotient is a 1-digit number and the estimated quotient gotten by rounding the divisor to the nearest ten works. Then they will divide again where the quotient is a 1-digit number, but the estimated quotient gotten by rounding the divisor to the nearest ten may be too big or too small. Then they will divide a 3-digit number by a 2-digit number where the quotient is a 2-digit number by first dividing tens, getting a remainder, and then combining the remainder with the ones and repeating the process. Finally, they will divide a 4-digit whole number by a 2-digit number using the same skills.

When trying an estimated quotient, the remainder must always be less than the divisor. If it is not, we make the quotient larger. We can also divide again.

For example, in 473 ÷ 78, we might estimate by rounding 78 to 80 and try 5 since 6 x 80 = 480, which is too large. The remainder, though, is larger than the divisor. So we change the quotient to 6 and try that. Or, we can divide again, and then add 5 and 1 to get 6 with a remainder of 5 as the answer.

$$
\begin{array}{r}
5 \\
7\,8\overline{)4\,7\,3} \\
\underline{3\,9\,0} \\
8\,3
\end{array}
$$

$$
\begin{array}{r}
6 \\
7\,8\overline{)4\,7\,3} \\
\underline{4\,6\,8} \\
5
\end{array}
$$

The division algorithm can be quite difficult for many students. Provide students with plenty of practice and guidance.

$$
\begin{array}{r}
1 \\
5 \\
7\,8\overline{)4\,7\,3} \\
\underline{3\,9\,0} \\
8\,3 \\
\underline{7\,8} \\
5
\end{array}
$$

Copyright © 2005 SingaporeMath.com Inc., Oregon

Activity 2.2a   **Divide by tens or a 2-digit number**

1. Discuss division by tens.
    • Refer to **(a) on p. 28 in the textbook**.
        ○ Remind students that we can divide by tens by first dividing by 10, and then by the digit in the tens place.

$$140 \div 20 = 140 \div 10 \div 2 = 14 \div 2 = 7$$

        ○ Method 1 shows $140 \div 20$ being done by removing 0's from both the total and the number being divided.
        ○ Method 2 shows the division being done by recognizing that $7 \times 20 = 140$.

    • Refer to **(b) on p. 28 of the textbook**.
        ○ Tell students that if we use method 1 here, we do not get the correct whole number remainder. $15 \div 2$ gives a remainder of 1, but the remainder for $150 \div 20$ is actually 10.
        ○ When there is a remainder, we can't just cross off 0's and divide. We have to do the division without removing 0's in order to get the correct remainder.
        ○ However, we can find the quotient using estimation. To estimate the answer to $150 \div 20$, we can find the answer to $140 \div 20$ (since 14 is the multiple of 2 closest to 15), solve $140 \div 20$ as $14 \div 2 = 7$, and use 7 as the quotient in the *original* problem. We use the original problem to find the correct remainder.

$$\begin{array}{r} 7 \ \text{r } 10 \\ 2\,0\,)\overline{1\,5\,0} \\ \underline{1\,4\,0} \ = 7 \times 20 \\ 1\,0 \end{array}$$

    • Discuss **task 1, textbook p. 29**.

        ○ (a): Estimate the quotient by looking at the tens. Find the multiple of 3 closest to 7 but smaller than 7. $3 \times 2 = 6$, $30 \times 2 = 60$. Use 2.

$$\begin{array}{r} 2 \ \ \text{r } 10 \\ 3\,0\,)\overline{7\,0} \\ \underline{6\,0} \\ 1\,0 \end{array}$$

        ○ (b): Estimate the quotient by looking at the tens. If we could cross out 0's, we would have $43 \div 6$. Think: $6 \times 7 = 42$, and $6 \times 8 = 56$, which is too large, so use 7 as the quotient. Multiply it by 60 to get 420 and subtract that from the total to get the remainder.

$$\begin{array}{r} 7 \ \text{r } 10 \\ 6\,0\,)\overline{4\,3\,0} \\ \underline{4\,2\,0} \\ 1\,0 \end{array}$$

        ○ (c): Estimate the quotient by looking at tens: $2 \times 4 = 8$. $2 \times 5 = 10$, which is too big. So use 4 as the quotient.

$$\begin{array}{r} 4 \ \ \text{r } 9 \\ 2\,0\,)\overline{8\,9} \\ \underline{8\,0} \\ 9 \end{array}$$

        ○ (d): Look at tens only to estimate the quotient. If we could cross out the last digit for both, we would have $62 \div 7$. $7 \times 8 = 56$, $7 \times 9 = 63$, which is too large. Use 8 as the quotient.

$$\begin{array}{r} 8 \ \text{r } 65 \\ 7\,0\,)\overline{6\,2\,5} \\ \underline{5\,6\,0} \\ 6\,5 \end{array}$$

        ○ Remember that the remainder needs to always be less than the divisor. If it is not, then make the quotient larger. Or, we can divide again. This idea will be developed more in Activity 2.2b.

    • Have students do **task 2, textbook p. 29**.

Copyright © 2005 SingaporeMath.com Inc., Oregon

2. Discuss division by a 2-digit number where the quotient is a 1-digit number.

- Discuss **task 3, textbook p. 29**.
  - Estimate the answer by rounding the divisor to 20, and then follow the same procedure as we used when dividing by tens. Imagine the ones crossed off, and then mentally find what number times 2 gives an answer closest to 7.
    2 x **3** = 6, so 20 x 3 = 60, which is less that 74. 2 x 4 = 8, so 4 would give too high a number (20 x 4 = 80).
  - Put 3 down as the quotient and multiply it by 21 to find the remainder by subtracting the product (63) from the total.

- Discuss **task 3, textbook p. 29**.
  - Estimate again by rounding the number we are dividing by to a ten. Round 47 to 50, then imaging the ones crossed off and find the multiple of 5 closest to 25: 5 x **5** = 25. So use 5 as the quotient.

- Have students do **task 5, textbook p. 29**.

Workbook Exercise 12, #1

Activity 2.2b   **More division**

1. Discuss division of a 2-digit number by a 2-digit number where the estimated quotient is too big or too small.

- Discuss **task 6, textbook p. 29**.
  - Round 24 to 20 and look at the tens to find an estimated quotient. 2 x 4 = 8 (20 x 4 = 80), whereas 2 x 5 = 10 (20 x 5 = 100), which is too large. So we try 4 as the quotient first. But 4 turns out to be too large, since 24 x 4 = 96, which is greater than 89. Try the number that is 1 less.

- Discuss **task 7, textbook p. 30**.
  - Round 26 to 30 and find how many times 3 goes into 7. 30 x 2 = 60, but 30 x 3 = 90, which is greater than 78. So we try 2 as a quotient. Multiply 26 by 2 and subtract the product from the dividend. The remainder is larger than the number we are dividing by (26), so the estimated quotient is too small. The remainder should never be larger than the number we are dividing by. So we try a number that is one more (3).
  - Note that if the estimated quotient is too small, rather than trying a larger quotient, we can divide again by subtracting another 26 from the remainder we found when trying out 2.

$$\begin{array}{r} 1 \\ 2 = 3 \\ \hline 26)\overline{78} \\ 52 \\ 26 \\ 26 \end{array}$$

  - You may also want to point out that sometimes we can find a better estimate if both the total and the divisor round in the same direction by rounding them both. Here, we could use 80 ÷ 30 and try 3 as the quotient.

- Have students do **task 8, textbook p. 30**.

Copyright © 2005 SingaporeMath.com Inc., Oregon

3. Discuss division of a 3-digit number by a 2-digit number where the estimated quotient is too big or too small.

- Discuss **task 9, textbook p. 30**.
  - ○ Round 33 to 30. 30 x 9 = 270, so try 9 as the quotient first. When we multiply 33 by 9, we get 297, which is too large. So we try 8.

- Discuss **task 10, textbook p. 30**.
  - ○ Round 78 to 80. 80 x 5 = 400, but 80 x 6 = 480, which is larger than 473. So try 5 as the quotient first. This turns out to be too small, so we try 6.
  - ○ If we try 5 first, and got a remainder that is larger than the divisor, we can subtract another 78 from the remainder and add 1 to the quotient.
  - ○ We could also estimate by rounding the total up as well, and use 480 ÷ 80 so we try 6 as the quotient.
  - ○ Point out that in whatever approach we use, we are trying to get the closest estimate. The estimate is often one too high or one too low, and there is no single rounding method that will always give us the exact quotient on the first try.

- Have students do **task 11, textbook p. 30**

Workbook Exercise 12, #2

Activity 2.2c   **Even more division**

1. Discuss division of a 3-digit whole number by a 2-digit whole number where the quotient may be a 2-digit number.

- Discuss **tasks 12, textbook p. 31**.
  - ○ Have students look at the division problems in tasks 10 and 11 on p. 30 again. Ask them to compare the first 2 digits of the total with the divisor. In 473 ÷ 78, we know that we can't divide 4 hundreds into 78 groups, so we have to rename them as tens. But 47 tens will not go into 78 groups either, and we need to rename the tens as ones so that we have 473 ones. We can put 5 ones each into 78 groups. In each of these problems the number formed by the first 2 digits, the hundreds and tens together, is smaller than the number we are dividing by. So we have to rename the entire total as ones in order to divide. The answer will only have ones.
  - ○ Now have them look at the problem in task 12 on p. 31. We can't divide 5 hundreds into 16 groups, but we can divide 57 tens into 16 groups. So the answer will have tens as well as ones.
  - ○ Step through this problem with your students. We do it in two steps.
    - ▪ Step 1: divide 57 tens by 16 and get a remainder. We could use 57 tens ÷ 20 to get an estimate of 2 (20 x 2 = 40 which is less than 57), which will be too small, so we can try 3 or divide again. Or, we an use an estimate of 60 tens ÷ 20 and try 3
    - ▪ Step 2: Rename the 9 tens as ones. We now have 90 ones to divide by 16.

- Work through the problems in **task 13, textbook p. 31** with students, discussing each step.
  - ○ (a): 8 hundreds cannot be divided into 34 groups, but 87 tens can. 80 ÷ 30 ≈ 2, so try 2 tens, which works. Rename the remainder as ones, add the 0 ones. We can then round 190 to 180. 18 tens ÷ 3 tens = 6 tens, so try 6, which proves to be too large, so we try 5.

Copyright © 2005 SingaporeMath.com Inc., Oregon

- o (b): We can estimate 86 tens ÷ 28 by 8 tens ÷ 3 tens ≈ 2 tens with a remainder. 2 is too small so we will have to divide again or try 3. (Or, we might have rounded the divisor up as well, using 9 tens ÷ 3 tens to give us 3 as the estimate.) The remainder of 22 ones can't be divided into 28, so we put 0 for ones in the quotient.

- o (c): 70 is greater than 47, so we first find the quotient for the tens. 70 tens ÷ 5 tens ≈ 1 ten, so try 1 first as the quotient for the tens. It works, and the remainder is 23 tens. 23 tens and 3 ones is 233 ones. Now divide 233 by 47. Since 50 x 4 = 200, try 4. 47 x 4 = 188, and 233 – 188 gives a remainder of 45. 4 worked, just barely.

$$\begin{array}{r} 14 \quad \text{r } 45 \\ 47\overline{)703} \\ \underline{47} \\ 233 \\ \underline{188} \\ 45 \end{array}$$

- o (d): Round 15 up to 20 and try 3 tens first. This will be too small, so we then try 4.

$$\begin{array}{r} 40 \quad \text{r } 12 \\ 15\overline{)612} \\ \underline{60} \\ 12 \end{array}$$

- Have students do **task 14, textbook p. 31**.

Workbook Exercise 13, #1

Activity 2.2d   **Divide a 4-digit number**

1. Discuss division of a 4-digit whole number by a 2-digit whole number.

- Guide students through the problems in **task 15, textbook p. 31**.
   - o (a): The first two digits of the dividend form the number 65, which is larger than the divisor 28, so the quotient will be a 3-digit number (we can divide 65 hundreds into 28 groups and need to find how many go in each group, and how many are left over). We do the problem in 3 steps. First we divide 65 hundreds by 28. The remainder is 9 hundreds. 9 hundreds and 5 tens is 95 tens. Divide 95 tens by 28. The remainder is 11 tens. 11 tens and 2 ones is 112. Divide 112 by 28.
   - o (b): The first two digits of the dividend form the number 43, which is smaller than the divisor 52. So the quotient will have 2 digits, and we start by dividing 432 tens by 52.
   - o (c): 68 is larger than 64. Start by dividing the hundreds. The remainder from dividing the hundreds is 4 hundreds. 4 hundreds and 2 tens is 42 tens. Since 42 tens is smaller than 64, the quotient will not have any tens. So we now have to rename the tens as ones and divide 420 ones by 64.

$$\begin{array}{r} 106 \quad \text{r } 36 \\ 64\overline{)6820} \\ \underline{64} \\ 420 \\ \underline{384} \\ 36 \end{array}$$

   - o (d): 31 is less than 45, so we start by dividing the tens by 45: 318 tens ÷ 45. The remainder from dividing the tens plus the ones is less than 45, so there are no ones in the quotient.

$$\begin{array}{r} 70 \quad \text{r } 35 \\ 45\overline{)3185} \\ \underline{315} \\ 35 \end{array}$$

- Provide some additional examples.

- Have students do **task 16, textbook p. 31**.

Workbook Exercise 13, #2

Copyright © 2005 SingaporeMath.com Inc., Oregon

Activity 2.2e   **Word problems**

1. Use **problems 1-6, Practice 2A, textbook p. 32** to review and practice division.
   - Provide students with plenty of ongoing practice in dividing a whole number by a 2-digit whole number. You can give them several problems each day or every few days.

2. Discuss **problem 7, Practice 2A, textbook p. 32**, and then discuss two variants involving remainders.

   - In problem 7, we divide 36 by 12 to get an answer of 3 cakes.

   - Discuss the following two problems:

     ➢ A baker has 500 eggs. He wants to make cakes and will use 12 eggs in each cake. How many cakes can he make?
       $500 \div 12 = 41$ R 8. He can make 41 cakes. The remaining 8 eggs are not used.

     ➢ A farmer has 500 eggs and wants to put them all in egg cartons. Each egg carton holds 12 eggs. How many egg cartons are needed?
       $500 \div 21 = 41$ R 8. He needs 42 cartons. Here, an additional egg carton is needed for the remainder. There are 41 filled cartons, and one more is needed for the rest of the eggs.

2. Have students do **problems 8-14, Practice 2A, textbook p. 32**.
   - Have students share their solutions and discuss any methods that differ. For example, problem 13 can be solved by dividing 70 by 14 to get the number of students on each team (5), then subtracting 2 from 5 to get the number of boys on each team. Multiplying 3 boys by 14 teams gives the total number of boys.
     Or, we can multiply 2 by 14 to get the total number of girls, subtract 28 from 70 to get the number of boys. The latter solution involves fewer steps.
   - Explain installment plans before students do problem 11.
   - Encourage students to draw models to solve these problems if they have trouble with any of them.

Activity 2.2f   **Review**

Notes for Review 1:
- Reviews in *Primary Mathematics* cover previous levels, as well as the current level. Many of the questions in **Review 1** in the **workbook** can be solved using concepts taught or reviewed so far with the first two units of Primary Mathematics 5A, but the review does cover some material taught in *Primary Mathematics 4*.
- Problem #11 in Review 1 deals with conversion of measurements. This will be reviewed later in this guide in part 4 of unit 2. You can use this problem to assess how much review will be needed, or save it to use during that review.
- Problems #15-18 and #22 in Review 1 deal with area and perimeter. Area and perimeter will be reviewed in this guide in Unit 5. You can assign these problems at that time.
- Problem #8 deals with factors and multiples. Use this session to review factors and multiples, since an understanding of factors and multiples is necessary for the next unit in *Primary Mathematics 5A* (Fractions). For a thorough review of factors and multiples,

Copyright © 2005 SingaporeMath.com Inc., Oregon

see *Primary Mathematics 4A*, Unit 1, Parts 3 and 4 and the accompanying section in the *Primary Mathematics Teacher's Guide 4A*.

1. Review factors.
   - Remind students that any whole number can be expressed as the product of two or more whole numbers, or factors. Since 4 x 3 = 12, then 4 and 3 are factors of 12.
   - Guide students in systematically listing the factors of 24 (problem 8.a in Review 1).
     - 1 is a factor of all whole numbers, and so is the number itself. They see that 2, 3 and 4 divide 24 evenly, while 5 does not. 6 has already been found as the factor to go with 4. So the factors of 24 are 1, 2, 3, 4, 6, 8, 12, and 24. Those are all the numbers that divide 24 exactly.

1 x 24 = 24
2 x 12 = 24
3 x 8 = 24
4 x 6 = 24
6 x 4 = 24
8 x 3 = 24
12 x 2 = 24
24 x 1 = 24

   - You may want to review divisibility rules, which can help in finding factors.
     - A number is divisible by 2 if the last digit is 0, 2, 4, 6, or 8.
     - A number is divisible by 5 if the last digit is 5 or 0.
     - A number is divisible by 3 if the sum of the digits is divisible by 3.
     - A number is divisible by 9 if the sum of the digits is divisible by 9.
     - A number is divisible by 4 if the last two digits are divisible by 4.
   - Remind students that the common factor of two numbers is any factor that both numbers have.
   - Have them find the common factors for 48 and 60 by first listing all the factors of each number. Point out that 12 is the highest common factor for 48 and 60.

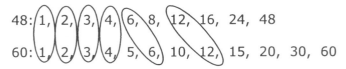

     48: 1, 2, 3, 4, 6, 8, 12, 16, 24, 48

     60: 1, 2, 3, 4, 5, 6, 10, 12, 15, 20, 30, 60

     1, 2, 3, 4, 6 and 12 are common factors of 48 and 60.

2. Review multiples.
   - Remind students that a multiple of a number is any number that is the product of the given number and a whole number. For example, 10 is a multiple of the given number 2 since 2 x 5 = 10. Since 2 x 5 = 10, we can say that 2 and 5 are factors of 10, and 10 is a multiple of 2 and a multiple of 5.
     - Usually we say the first multiple of any number is that number x 1, the second multiple is that number x 2, and so on.
     - Have students find the first 12 multiples of 6 (problem 8.b of review 1). They can simply count by 6's. 6, 12, 18, 24, 30, 36, 42, 48, 54, 60, 66, 72.
   - Remind students that a common multiple of two numbers is any multiple that both numbers have.
     - Have students list the first 12 multiples of 8 (8, 16, 24, 32, 40, 48, 56, 64, 72, 80, 88, 96, and find any multiples that are common to both (24, 48, 72).
     - Point out that 24 is the least common multiple of 6 and 8.
     - Ask students if they know a good way to find any common multiple of 2 numbers. They can simply multiply the two numbers together. 6 x 8 = 48, and 48 is a common multiple of both 6 and 8.
     - Ask students to find the first 3 common multiples of 3, 4, and 6 by listing multiples. Point out once they find the first common multiple, the rest are just multiples of the first.

Copyright © 2005 SingaporeMath.com Inc., Oregon

    o   Tell student that one way to find the least common multiple of a several number is to first look at all the largest number to see if it is a multiple of the others. For example, 9 is a common multiple of 3 and 9. But it is not a common multiple of 3, 6, and 9. If the largest number is not a multiple, try the largest number multiplied by 2. For example, 9 x 2 = 18, and 18 is a common multiple for 2, 6, and 9. If the largest number multiplied by 1 or 2 is not a multiple of the others, try multiplying it by 3 and check that product. And so on.

3. Problems #19-21 could be done in class so that students can share their solutions. Possible solutions are shown here:

19.   Money for 25 melons = 25 x $6 = $150
     Remaining melons = 45 - 25 = 20
     Money for remaining melons = 20 x $4 = $80
     Total money = $150 + $80 = $230

20.   Total money spent
     = $295 + $65 + $65
     = $425
     Change = $500 - $425 = $75

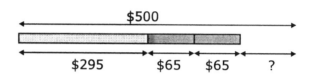

21.   Number of stamps Jane has
     = 278 + 64
     = 342
     Number of stamps Sam has
     = 500 - Jane's stamps
     = 500 - 342
     = 158
     [3d edition: Brandy is Lihua and Sam is Samy]

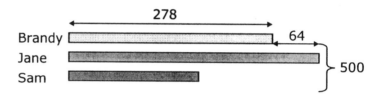

Copyright © 2005 SingaporeMath.com Inc., Oregon

Unit 3 – Fractions

Objectives

- Associate division with fractions.
- Change an improper fraction to a whole number or mixed number using division.
- Add and subtract unlike fractions.
- Add and subtract mixed fractions.
- Multiply a fraction by a whole number.
- Convert a measurement expressed as a fraction or as a mixed number to a smaller unit or to a compound unit.
- Express a part of a measurement as a fraction of the whole.
- Multiply a fraction by a fraction.
- Divide a fraction by a whole number.
- Solve multi-step word problems involving fractions.

Suggested number of sessions: 21

	Objectives	Textbook	Workbook	Activities
Part 1 : Fraction and Division				**3 sessions**
28	▪ Review equivalent fractions, simplest form, improper factions, and mixed numbers.			3.1a
29	▪ Associate division with fractions. ▪ Change an improper number to a mixed number or to a whole number by division. Express the quotient as a whole number or mixed number.	pp. 33-34 pp. tasks 1-4	Ex. 14	3.1b
30	▪ Practice. ▪ Solve word problems involving division where the answer is a mixed number.	p. 36, Practice 3A		3.1c
Part 2 : Addition and Subtraction of Unlike Fractions				**3 sessions**
31	▪ Add unlike fractions.	p. 37 p. 38, tasks 1-4	Ex. 15	3.2a
32	▪ Subtract unlike fractions.	p. 39, tasks 5-8	Ex. 16	3.2b
33	▪ Review. ▪ Solve simple word problems involving the addition and subtraction of unlike fractions.	p. 40, Practice 3B		3.2c
Part 3 : Addition and Subtraction of Mixed Numbers				**2 sessions**
34	▪ Add mixed numbers.	p. 41 p. 42, task 1	Ex. 17	3.3a
35	▪ Subtract mixed numbers. ▪ Solve simple word problems involving the addition and subtraction of mixed numbers.	p. 42, tasks 2-3 p. 43, Practice 3C	Ex. 18	3.3b

Copyright © 2005 SingaporeMath.com Inc., Oregon

	Objectives	Textbook	Workbook	Activities
Part 4 : Product of a Fraction and a Whole Number				**4 sessions**
36	▪ Multiply a proper fraction by a whole number.	pp. 44-45, tasks 1-2 p. 48, Practice 3D, 1-3		3.4a
37	▪ Convert a fraction of a measurement to a smaller unit of measurement by multiplying by a conversion factor.	pp. 46-47, tasks 3-7	Ex. 19	3.4b
38	▪ Convert a measurement expressed as a mixed number to a smaller unit of measurement.	p. 47, tasks 7-9 p. 48, Practice 3D, 4-9	Ex. 20	3.4c
39	▪ Express a part of a quantity as a fraction. ▪ Solve simple word problems	p. 47, task 10 p. 48, Practice 3D, 10-13	Ex. 21	3.4d
Part 5 : Product of Fractions				**3 sessions**
40	▪ Illustrate a fraction of a fraction with rectangular grids or fraction discs.	p. 49 pp. 50-51, tasks 1-5		3.5a
41	▪ Multiply a fraction by a fraction.	p. 51, tasks 5-6	Ex. 22	3.5b
42	▪ Practice. ▪ Solve simple word problems.	p. 52, Practice 3E	Ex. 23	3.5c
Part 6 : Dividing a Fraction by a Whole Number				**2 sessions**
43	▪ Illustrate a fraction divided by a whole number with rectangular grids or fraction discs. ▪ Divide a fraction by a whole number.	p. 53 p. 54, tasks 1-3	Ex. 24	3.6a
44	▪ Practice. ▪ Solve simple word problems.	p. 55, Practice 3F	Ex. 25	3.6b
Part 7 : Word Problems				**4 sessions**
45	▪ Solve multi-step word problems involving fraction of a set or the value of a fractional part of the whole, using part-whole model diagrams.	p. 56 p. 57, tasks 1-3	Ex. 26	3.7a
46		p. 60, Practice 3G, 1, 2, and 4	Ex. 27	3.7b
47	▪ Solve multi-step word problems involving fractions of a remainder of a fraction of a whole, using part-whole model diagrams.	p. 58-59, task 4-6	Ex. 28	3.7c
48	▪ Practice.	p. 60, Practice 3G, 3, 5-8	Ex. 29	3.7d

Copyright © 2005 SingaporeMath.com Inc., Oregon

Part 1: Fractions and Division	3 sessions

Objectives

- Review improper fractions and mixed numbers.
- Associate division with fractions.
- Change an improper fraction to a mixed number or to a whole number by division.
- Express the quotient as a whole number or as a mixed number.

Materials

- Paper circles

Homework

- Workbook Exercise 14

Notes

By now, students have an intuitive understanding of the connection between fractions and division. In *Primary Mathematics 4A*, they found the fraction of a set by dividing the set into equal parts, e.g., to find half of 24, they divided 24 into 2 equal parts. In this section, the association between division and fractions is introduced formally.

In *Primary Mathematics 4A*, students learned to convert from improper fractions to mixed numbers and vice versa by finding the number of fractional parts that made wholes. For example: $\frac{21}{4} = \frac{20}{4} + \frac{1}{4} = 5\frac{1}{4}$.

In this section, students will learn how to use division to change an improper fraction to a whole number, and to express the remainder as a fraction of the divisor: $\frac{21}{4} = 21 \div 4 = 5\frac{1}{4}$.

$$\begin{array}{r} 5 \\ 4\overline{)21} \\ 20 \\ \hline 1 \end{array}$$

Students should have a good understanding of equivalent fractions, comparing fractions, mixed numbers, and improper fractions. This is reviewed briefly in Activity 3.1a. If more review is required, refer to *Primary Mathematics 3B* textbook, Unit 6 and *Primary Mathematics Teacher's Guide 3B*, and *Primary Mathematics 4A* textbook, Unit 3, Parts 3 and 4, and *Primary Mathematics Teacher's Guide 4A*.

As you teach this unit, you may want to simultaneously review earlier material by giving students several questions at the beginning of each class. You can use problems 1-14 and 28-34 of Review A, textbook pp. 61-64.

Students should know the terms numerator and denominator. If the still have trouble remembering which is which, say "top" along with "numerator" and "bottom" along with "denominator" in discussions so that they are sure to understand the discussion.

Copyright © 2005 SingaporeMath.com Inc., Oregon

Activity 3.1a   **Fractions**

1. Review equivalent fractions, and writing fractions in their simplest form.

   - Write two fractions on the board, such as $\frac{1}{3}$ and $\frac{2}{6}$, and ask

     students if they are equivalent.
     - Remind students that equivalent fractions are fractions that
       mean the same thing. You can draw fraction bars or fraction
       discs to show that these two are equivalent.
   - Ask students how we find equivalent fractions.
     - We can multiply the numerator and denominator by the
       same number to get an equivalent fraction.
     - We can divide the numerator and denominator by the same
       number to get an equivalent fraction.
   - Ask which of these fractions is in simplest form.
     - Remind students that *simplest form* is a term we use when there is no common
       factor (other than 1, which doesn't change the fraction) that can divide both the top
       (numerator) and bottom (denominator) of a fraction. As long as both the numerator
       and denominator can still be divided by the same number, the fraction is not in
       simplest form.

2. Review proper fraction, improper fraction, mixed numbers, and the conversion of a mixed
   number into an improper fraction and vice versa.

   - Write several fractions on the board, such as $\frac{5}{7}$, $\frac{8}{8}$, $\frac{17}{12}$, and $6\frac{2}{3}$ and ask students to

     identify which are proper fractions, improper fraction, or mixed numbers.
     - Remind students that in a proper fraction, the value is less than 1, and the
       numerator (top) is smaller than the denominator (bottom).
     - In an improper fraction, the value is equal to or greater than 1, and the numerator
       (top) is equal to or greater than the denominator (bottom).
     - A mixed number has both a whole number part and a fraction part.

   - Write a mixed number on the board, such as $6\frac{2}{3}$, and ask students to write it as an

     improper fraction.
     - Remind them that we can find the equivalent fraction for 6 with 3 in the denominator

       (bottom) and then add: $6\frac{2}{3} = \frac{18}{3} + \frac{2}{3} = \frac{20}{3}$.
     - Essentially, we are multiplying the whole number 6 by the denominator 3, adding the
       product to the numerator, and writing the sum over the denominator:

       $6\frac{2}{3} = \frac{(6 \times 3) + 2}{3} = \frac{20}{3}$. Students can do this mentally.

   - Write an improper fraction where the numerator is a
     multiple of the denominator. $\frac{15}{5} = 3$
     - Ask students for the whole number.
     - Then write another improper fraction, increasing the $\frac{17}{5} = \frac{15}{5} + \frac{2}{5} = 3\frac{2}{5}$
       numerator to less than the next multiple. Ask students
       to write it as a mixed number.

Copyright © 2005 SingaporeMath.com Inc., Oregon

3. Review renaming mixed numbers.
   - Remind students that we can rename whole numbers. For example, we can rename 25, which represents 2 tens 5 ones, as 1 ten 15 ones. Similarly, we can rename mixed numbers.
   - Write a problem such as $2\frac{1}{3} = 1\frac{?}{3}$. Lead students to see that they can rename one of the whole numbers as $\frac{3}{3}$ and add it to $\frac{1}{3}$.
   - Discuss a mental math method: We simply reduce the whole number by 1, and add the numerator to the denominator and use that as the new numerator.
   - Provide some additional examples. Write some mixed numbers and ask the students to rename it so that the whole number part is one less.

$$2\frac{1}{3} = 1\frac{?}{3}$$

$$2\frac{1}{3} = 2 + \frac{1}{3}$$

$$= 1 + 1 + \frac{1}{3}$$

$$= 1 + \frac{3}{3} + \frac{1}{3}$$

$$= 1\frac{4}{3}$$

$$4\frac{1}{6} = 3\frac{7}{6}$$

$$8\frac{2}{3} = 7\frac{5}{3}$$

4. Provide students with some problems for practice.
   You can have them do **problems 15-18, and 20-23, Review A, textbook pp. 62-63**.

Activity 3.1b   **Fractions and Division**

1. Discuss the relationship between fractions and division.
   - Divide students into groups of 4 and give each group one large paper circle, which represents a pizza or other circular food. Have them divide the pizza so they each get the same amount.
   - Write 1 ÷ 4. Tell students we have 1 pizza and want to divide it among 4 students. Each student would get $\frac{1}{4}$.

   $1 \div 4$

   $1 \div 4 = \frac{1}{4}$

   - Give each group of 4 students 9 paper circles. Tell them they now have 9 pizzas that they must divide evenly among themselves.
   - Write 9 ÷ 4. Now we have 9 pizzas, and we want to divide it equally among 4 students.

   $9 \div 4 = \frac{9}{4} = 2\frac{1}{4}$

   - We could divide each pizza into fourths. We would have 36 fourths. If we then divide up the 36 quarters of pizzas among the 4 students. Each student would get 9 pieces. Since each piece is a fourth, each person gets $\frac{9}{4}$, nine fourths, or 2 whole pieces and a fourth, $2\frac{1}{4}$.
   - Or, we could give each student 2 pizzas, using 8 of them, with 1 remaining pizza left over. Then we can divide the remainder into fourths and put a fourth in each group. Write $9 \div 4 = 2\frac{1}{4}$.

   $9 \div 4 = 2\frac{1}{4}$

   - Show 9 ÷ 4 as a vertical division problem. The remainder is 1. We can divide the remainder as well by dividing it by 4. We show this as a fraction. So $9 \div 4 = 2 \text{ R } 1 = 2\frac{1}{4}$.

   $$\begin{array}{r} 2 \\ 4\overline{)9} \\ \underline{8} \\ 1 \end{array}$$

Copyright © 2005 SingaporeMath.com Inc., Oregon

- Ask students to convert the mixed number answer to an improper fraction. Point out that $9 \div 4 = \frac{9}{4}$.

$$9 \div 4 = 2\frac{1}{4} = \frac{9}{4}$$

- We can write any division problem as a fraction, and then convert it into a mixed number. Or we can perform the division and then divide the remainder as well. The quotient from dividing the remainder is the fraction, with the remainder in the numerator (top) and the number we are dividing by in the denominator (bottom).

2. Discuss **textbook pp. 33-34** and **tasks 1-3, textbook pp. 34-35**.

3. Have students do **task 4, textbook p. 35**.
   - You can ask a pair of students to show each problem on the board using different methods.

Workbook Exercise 14

Activity 3.1c   **Word Problems**

1. Have students do **Practice 3A, textbook p. 36** and share their solutions. Encourage them to draw models for the problems.

Copyright © 2005 SingaporeMath.com Inc., Oregon

| **Part 2: Addition and Subtraction of Unlike Fractions** | **3 sessions** |

Objectives

- Add unlike fractions.
- Subtract unlike fractions.

Materials

- Fraction discs

Homework

- Workbook Exercise 15
- Workbook Exercise 16

Notes

In *Primary Mathematics 4A*, students learned to add or subtract like or related fractions. *Like fractions* are fractions where the denominators are the same. *Related fractions* are fractions where the denominator of one fraction is a simple multiple of the denominator of the other fraction. Addition and subtraction will involve finding an equivalent fraction of only one of them. For example, $\dfrac{3}{4} + \dfrac{1}{8} = \dfrac{6}{8} + \dfrac{1}{8} = \dfrac{7}{8}$.

In this part students will learn to add and subtract unlike fractions where the denominator of one is not a simple multiple of the denominator of the other. So addition and subtraction will involve finding equivalent fractions of both. For example, $\dfrac{3}{8} + \dfrac{5}{6} = \dfrac{9}{24} + \dfrac{20}{24} = \dfrac{29}{24} = 1\dfrac{5}{24}$.

In this example, the equivalent fractions have a denominator that is the least common multiple of both 8 and 6. Of course, any equivalent fractions where the denominators are the same can be used, such as the product of the denominators of each fraction. In that case, equivalent fractions can be obtained by multiplying the numerator and denominator of each fraction by the denominator of the other fraction:
$$\frac{3}{8} + \frac{5}{6} = \frac{3 \times 6}{8 \times 6} + \frac{5 \times 8}{6 \times 8} = \frac{18}{48} + \frac{40}{48} = \frac{58}{48} = \frac{29}{24} = 1\frac{5}{24}.$$

Keep in mind that using the least common multiple of both denominators reduces the need for simplification at the end, and involves smaller numbers, making calculations easier.

Students should reduce answers to their simplest form. Answers that are improper fractions do not necessarily have to be converted to proper fractions. In high school, students will learn that it is better to keep intermediate answers as improper fractions. At this stage, however, students can visualize mixed numbers more easily than improper fractions, so you may want to require your students to convert all answers to proper fractions or mixed numbers.

The least common multiple of the denominators is also called the least common denominator.

Copyright © 2005 SingaporeMath.com Inc., Oregon

Activity 3.2a   **Add unlike fractions**

1. If you have not reviewed factors and multiples, do so at this time. See Activity 2.2e in this guide.

2. Review addition of like and related fractions.
   - Write an addition problem involving like fractions, such as $\frac{5}{8}+\frac{7}{8}$ and ask students to find the sum. Since the size of each part is the same, we simply add the number of parts. Remind students that they should put the final answer into its lowest term, as a proper fraction or mixed number.
   - Write an addition problem involving related fractions, such as $\frac{3}{4}+\frac{1}{8}$. Draw two fraction bars or discs illustrating these fractions.
   - Remind students that to add them, we need to make the parts the same size. To do this, we need to cut up the larger pieces into smaller pieces. If we cut each fourth in half, we have $\frac{6}{8}$. $\frac{6}{8}$ is an equivalent fraction of $\frac{3}{4}$. We can add 6 eighth pieces to 1 eighth piece to get 7 eighth pieces.

$$\frac{5}{8}+\frac{7}{8}=\frac{12}{8}$$
$$=\frac{3}{2}$$
$$=1\frac{1}{2}$$

$$\frac{3}{4}+\frac{1}{8}=?$$

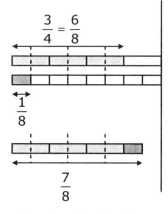

$$\frac{3}{4}+\frac{1}{8}=\frac{6}{8}+\frac{1}{8}=\frac{7}{8}$$

3. Discuss addition of unlike fractions.
   - Write an addition problem involving unrelated fractions, such as $\frac{3}{4}+\frac{1}{3}$. Draw fraction bars or discs for these.
   - Tell students that in order to add these, we again have to have parts of equal sizes, but we can't do this by simply dividing up the larger pieces. We have to divide each size piece so that we have equal sizes for both. We can figure out how we should divide each piece by finding a common multiple of the denominators, 4 and 3. 12 is a common multiple. If we divide up the whole into twelfths, each larger piece (each third) needs to be divided into 4 smaller pieces, so there will be 4 times as many, and each smaller piece (each fourth) needs to be divided into 3 smaller pieces, so there will be 3 times as many. Now both fraction bars are divided into fourths, and we can add the parts together.
   - In summary, to add unlike fractions, we have find equivalent fractions for both fractions; their denominators have to be the same.

$$\frac{3}{4}+\frac{1}{3}=?$$

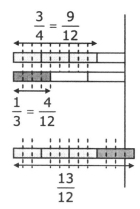

$$\frac{3}{4}+\frac{1}{3}=\frac{9}{12}+\frac{4}{12}=\frac{13}{12}=1\frac{1}{12}$$

Copyright © 2005 SingaporeMath.com Inc., Oregon

4. Discuss **textbook p. 37**.

5. Discuss three methods for finding equivalent fractions so that we can add unlike fractions.
    *   Refer to **task 1, textbook p. 38.** Discuss three methods. (In order to add two fractions together, both need to have a common denominator. Multiplying the two denominators together will always give a common denominator. If this, however, is not the least common denominator, it is worth looking for that since it often makes the problem simpler to compute mentally and requires less simplification at the end.)

    1. Multiply the two denominators together and use that to find equivalent fractions. $8 \times 6 = 24$. To find the equivalent fractions, we multiply both the numerator and denominator of $\frac{3}{8}$ by 6 and the numerator and denominator of $\frac{1}{6}$ by 8.

    $$\frac{3}{8} + \frac{1}{6} = \frac{3 \times 6}{8 \times 6} + \frac{1 \times 8}{6 \times 8}$$
    $$= \frac{18}{48} + \frac{8}{48}$$
    $$= \frac{26}{48} = \frac{13}{24}$$

    2. List equivalent fractions for the fraction with the greatest denominator until we get to one where we recognize the denominator as a multiple of the fraction with the smaller denominator. ($\frac{3}{8}, \frac{6}{16}, \frac{9}{24}$, 24 is a multiple of 6) Find the equivalent fraction of the fraction with the smaller denominator with that denominator ($\frac{1}{6} = \frac{?}{24}$, we need to multiply 6 by 4 to get 24, so multiply 1 by 4, $\frac{1}{6} = \frac{4}{24}$). Add the two equivalent fractions.

    3. Find the least common multiple of the denominators. This method is essentially the same as the first method and will give the same number in the color patches. Find the least common multiple of 6 and 8. We can do this by listing the common multiples of 6 and 8 until the same number appears in both lists. Or, we can list the multiples of the larger number (8) until we recognize one (24) as a multiple of the smaller number (6). Convert both fractions into equivalent fractions with 24 as the denominator. Add the two equivalent fractions.

    *   Discuss and compare each of the three methods for **tasks 2-3, textbook p. 38**. Students should realize that in order to add the fractions, they need to have the same denominator, but any common denominator can be used. Multiplying the two denominators together always gives a common denominator, but finding the least common denominator makes the computation easier and reduces the amount of simplification required to find the simplest term for the answer. (In later grades students will be adding and subtracting fractional algebraic expressions, where using the least common denominator will simplify the problem significantly).

6. Have students do **task 4, textbook p. 38**.

7. (Optional) Discuss an alternate method for adding like fractions whose sum is more than 1.
    *   Tell students that we can "make ones" by taking off one fraction whatever is needed to bring the other fraction to a one.
        o   Write $\frac{7}{8} + \frac{6}{8}$ on the board and show how we can add $\frac{7}{8}$ and $\frac{6}{8}$ by taking one eighth from $\frac{6}{8}$ to make a whole with $\frac{7}{8}$, leaving $\frac{5}{8}$.

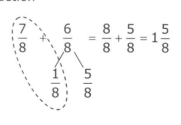

Copyright © 2005 SingaporeMath.com Inc., Oregon

- Have students try this method with the problems in task 4. This method is shown here for 4.(c)

$$\frac{3}{10} + \frac{5}{6} = \frac{9}{30} + \frac{25}{30} = \frac{4}{30} + \frac{30}{30} = 1\frac{4}{30} = 1\frac{2}{15}$$

$$\frac{4}{30} \quad \frac{5}{30}$$

Workbook exercise 15

Activity 3.2b   **Subtract unlike fractions**

1. Review subtraction of like and related fractions.

   - Write a subtraction problem involving related fractions, such as $\frac{3}{4} - \frac{1}{2}$.

   - Remind students that, as with addition of fractions, in order to subtract one fraction from another, the denominators have to be the same. In this problem we can change $\frac{1}{2}$ into a fraction with a denominator of 4.

$$\frac{3}{4} - \frac{1}{2} = \frac{3}{4} - \frac{2}{4}$$
$$= \frac{1}{4}$$

2. Discuss subtraction of unlike fractions.

   - Write a subtraction problem involving unlike fractions, such as $\frac{7}{10} - \frac{1}{6}$.

   - Tell students that, as with addition, we need to have the fractions the same size in order to subtract parts. Here, we have to find equivalent fractions for both factions, not just one of them. We use the same methods used with addition.
     - List equivalent fractions for the fraction with the greatest denominator until we get to one where we recognize the denominator as a multiple of the fraction with the smaller denominator. ($\frac{7}{10}$, $\frac{14}{20}$, $\frac{21}{30}$, 30 is a multiple of 6) Find the equivalent fraction of the fraction with the smaller denominator with that denominator ($\frac{1}{6} = \frac{?}{30}$, we need to multiply the denominator 6 by 5 to get 30, and so multiply the numerator 1 by 5 as well; $\frac{1}{6} = \frac{5}{30}$). Subtract the two equivalent fractions.

$$\frac{7}{10} - \frac{1}{6} = \frac{21}{30} - \frac{5}{30}$$
$$= \frac{16}{30}$$
$$= \frac{8}{15}$$

     - Or, first find the least common multiple of the denominators. We can do this by listing multiples of 10 until we recognize one as a also a multiple of 6. (30) Convert both fractions into equivalent fractions with 24 as the denominator. Add the two equivalent fractions.
     - Or, multiply the two denominators together and use that to find equivalent fractions. 10 x 6 = 60. To find the equivalent fractions, we multiply both the numerator and denominator of $\frac{7}{10}$ by 6 and the numerator and denominator of $\frac{1}{6}$ by 10.

$$\frac{7}{10} - \frac{1}{6} = \frac{7 \times 6}{10 \times 6} - \frac{1 \times 10}{6 \times 10}$$
$$= \frac{42}{60} - \frac{10}{60}$$
$$= \frac{32}{60}$$
$$= \frac{8}{15}$$

Copyright © 2005 SingaporeMath.com Inc., Oregon

3. Discuss **tasks 5-7, textbook p. 39.**

4. (Optional) Discuss an alternate method for subtracting like fractions when we are subtracting from a number greater than 1.

- Use task 7. Rather than converting $1\frac{7}{10}$ to an improper fraction and subtracting from that, we can subtract from the 1. In $1\frac{21}{30}$, there are not enough thirtieths to subtract $\frac{25}{30}$ from, so subtract from the 1, and then add on the remaining thirtieths. Students have learned as early as *Primary Mathematics 2B* how to "make a whole" with a fraction, but if necessary, convert the 1 to $\frac{30}{30}$.

$$1\frac{7}{10} - \frac{5}{6} = 1\frac{21}{30} - \frac{25}{30} = \frac{21}{30} + \frac{5}{30} = \frac{26}{30} = \frac{13}{15}$$

$$\underset{\frac{21}{30} \quad 1}{\diagup\diagdown}$$

- If we see that $\frac{5}{6}$ is larger than $\frac{7}{10}$ before finding equivalent fractions, we can subtract $\frac{5}{6}$ from 1 before converting the fractions.
- You can have students try this method with tasks 8.(b) and 8.(c). 8.(c) is shown here.

$$1\frac{7}{10} - \frac{5}{6} = \frac{7}{10} + \frac{1}{6} = \frac{21}{30} + \frac{5}{30} = \frac{26}{30} = \frac{13}{15}$$

$$\underset{\frac{7}{10} \quad 1}{\diagup\diagdown}$$

Workbook Exercise 16

Activity 3.2c   **Word Problems**

1. Have students do **Practice 3B, textbook p. 40** and share their solutions. Although these problems probably do not need to be modeled, if students have difficulty determining whether they need to add or subtract have them draw a part-whole model.

Copyright © 2005 SingaporeMath.com Inc., Oregon

Part 3: Addition and Subtraction of Mixed Numbers	**2 sessions**

Objectives

- Add mixed numbers.
- Subtract mixed numbers.

Materials

- Fraction discs or bars.

Homework

- Workbook Exercise 17
- Workbook Exercise 18

Notes

In this section students will learn to add and subtract mixed numbers.

The process for adding two (or more) mixed numbers involves the following steps:

Add the whole number parts.

$$3\frac{1}{2} + 6\frac{3}{4} = 3 + 6 + \frac{1}{2} + \frac{3}{4}$$
$$= 9 + \frac{1}{2} + \frac{3}{4}$$

Change the fractional parts to like fractions.

$$= 9 + \frac{2}{4} + \frac{3}{4}$$

Add the fractional parts.

$$= 9 + \frac{5}{4}$$

Write the answer in simplest form if necessary.

$$= 9 + 1\frac{1}{4}$$
$$= 10\frac{1}{4}$$

The process for subtracting mixed numbers involves similar steps:

Subtract the whole number parts.

$$5\frac{1}{6} - 2\frac{5}{9} = 3\frac{1}{6} - \frac{5}{9}$$

Change the fractional parts to like fractions.

$$= 3\frac{3}{18} - \frac{10}{18}$$

Rename the part of the mixed number if its fractional part is not enough to subtract from.

$$= 2\frac{21}{18} - \frac{10}{18}$$

Subtract the fraction parts.
Write the answer in simplest form.

$$= 2\frac{11}{18}$$

Copyright © 2005 SingaporeMath.com Inc., Oregon

Activity 3.3a   **Add mixed numbers**

1. Illustrate addition of mixed numbers.

    - Write an addition problem, such as $2\frac{1}{2} + 1\frac{3}{4}$.

    - Use fraction discs or bars to illustrate the addition process:

$$2\frac{1}{2} + 1\frac{3}{4} = 2 + \frac{1}{2} + 1 + \frac{3}{4}$$ Add the whole number parts.

$$= 3 + \frac{1}{2} + \frac{3}{4}$$

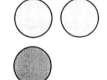

$$= 3 + \frac{2}{4} + \frac{3}{4}$$ Change the fractional parts to like fractions.

$$= 3 + \frac{5}{4}$$ Add the fractional parts.

$$= 3 + 1\frac{1}{4}$$ Write the answer in simplest form.

$$= 4\frac{1}{4}$$

    - Refer to **textbook p. 41** and **task 1, textbook p. 42**. Guide students through the addition process for these problems. Use fraction discs or bars to illustrate the process. For example:

    (a) $3\frac{5}{8} + 1\frac{7}{12} = 3 + \frac{5}{8} + 1 + \frac{7}{12}$

$$= 4\frac{5}{8} + \frac{7}{12}$$ Add the whole numbers together.

$$= 4\frac{15}{24} + \frac{14}{24}$$ Change eighths and twelfths to twenty-fourths.

$$= 4\frac{29}{24} \quad \text{or} \quad 4\frac{5}{24} + \frac{24}{24}$$ Add like fractions.

$$= 5\frac{5}{24}$$ Simplify.

2. Provide additional practice.
    - Have students do **problems 1 and 3 of Practice 3C, textbook p. 43**.

Workbook Exercise 17

___

Copyright © 2005 SingaporeMath.com Inc., Oregon

Activity 3.3b   **Subtract mixed numbers**

1. Illustrate subtraction of mixed numbers.
   - Write a subtraction problem, such as $4\frac{1}{2} - 1\frac{3}{4}$.
   - Use fraction discs or bars to illustrate the subtraction process:

$4\frac{1}{2} - 1\frac{3}{4} = 3\frac{1}{2} - \frac{3}{4}$	Subtract the whole number parts.	
$= 3\frac{2}{4} - \frac{3}{4}$	Change the fractional parts to like fractions.	
$= 2\frac{6}{4} - \frac{3}{4}$	Rename part of the mixed number if its fractional part is not enough to subtract.	
$= 2\frac{3}{4}$	Subtract fractional parts. Simplify if necessary.	

   - Refer to **tasks 2-3, textbook p. 42**. Guide students through the subtraction process for these problems. Use fraction discs or bars to illustrate the process.

2. Have students do **Practice 3C, textbook p. 43** for additional practice in adding and subtracting mixed numbers.
   - Have students share their solutions for the word problems. These problems do not have to be modeled except perhaps using a part-whole model if there is confusion over whether to add or subtract.

Workbook Exercise 18

Copyright © 2005 SingaporeMath.com Inc., Oregon

Part 4: Product of a Fraction and a Whole Number   4 sessions

Objectives

- Multiply a fraction by a whole number.
- Convert a measurement expressed as a fraction or as a mixed number to a smaller unit or a compound unit.
- Express a part of a measurement as a fraction of the whole.

Materials

- Fraction discs or bars.

Homework

- Workbook Exercise 19
- Workbook Exercise 20
- Workbook Exercise 21

Notes

Students learned to multiply a proper fraction by a whole number in *Primary Mathematics 4A*. This is reviewed here and extended to mixed numbers in the context of conversion of measurement.

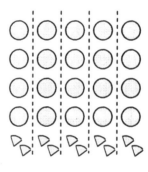

To find $\frac{3}{5}$ of 22, we can divide 20 of the 22 objects into 5 equal groups, and then the remaining two objects into five equal groups by putting $\frac{2}{5}$ of each into each of the 5 groups. There are $4\frac{2}{5}$ in each part. In three parts there are

$$3 \times 4\frac{2}{5} = 3 \times 4 + 3 \times \frac{2}{5} = 12 + \frac{6}{5} = 12 + 1\frac{1}{5} = 13\frac{1}{5}.$$

Students also learned to interpret $\frac{3}{5}$ of 20 as $\frac{3}{5} \times 20 = \frac{3 \times 20}{5}$. The computation is usually simplified by first finding an equivalent fraction for $\frac{20}{5}$. $\frac{3 \times 20}{5} = \frac{3 \times \overset{4}{\cancel{20}}}{\underset{1}{\cancel{5}}} = 3 \times 4 = 12$.

In *Primary Mathematics 3B*, students learned to convert measurement involving whole numbers. Here, students will learn to convert measurements involving fractions. They need to be familiar with conversion units, or how many smaller units equal a larger unit, such as 1 kg = 1000 g, 1 yd = 3 ft, 1 minute = 60 seconds) To convert from a larger unit to a smaller unit, we multiply by the conversion unit. For example, $\frac{1}{2}$ year = $\frac{1}{2}$ x 12 months = 6 months.

Copyright © 2005 SingaporeMath.com Inc., Oregon

Students learned in *Primary Mathematics 4A* to express a smaller part as a fraction of a total amount. The smaller part is expressed in a smaller unit of measurement, while the larger part is 1 unit of a larger measurement. For example, they learned to express 10 minutes as a fraction of 1 hour. This is reviewed here and extended to multiples of a whole unit, such as expressing 10 minutes as a fraction of 2 hours.

In order to express one measurement as a fraction of another, both must be in the same unit. Convert the larger unit of measure to the smaller unit of measure. For example, to express 10 minutes as a fraction of 2 hours, change 2 hours to 120 minutes. 10 minutes is $\frac{10}{120}$, or $\frac{1}{12}$ of 2 hours.

Copyright © 2005 SingaporeMath.com Inc., Oregon

Activity 3.4a

Fraction of a whole number

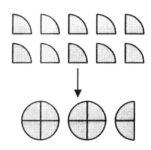

1. Discuss ways of multiplying a fraction by a whole number.

    *   Use or draw fraction discs to illustrate $10 \times \frac{1}{4}$.

        o   Tell students we can interpret $10 \times \frac{1}{4}$ to mean ten $\frac{1}{4}$'s, or ten fourths. $10 \times \frac{1}{4} = \frac{10}{4} = 2\frac{1}{2}$.

        o   We can first simplify $\frac{10}{4}$. We can show that we are simplifying $\frac{10}{4}$ by crossing out (canceling) and writing the numbers for the simplest form:

        $$\frac{1}{4} \times 10 = \frac{\cancel{10}^{5}}{\cancel{4}_{2}} = \frac{5}{2} = 2\frac{1}{2}$$

    *   Use the fraction discs to illustrate $\frac{1}{4} \times 10$, or $\frac{1}{4}$ of 10.

        o   Tell students that we can think of $10 \times \frac{1}{4}$ as $\frac{1}{4}$ **of** 10. We split 10 into four groups by putting 2 wholes into each group and, by dividing the remaining 2 wholes into halves, putting 1 of the halves into each group. This gives us the same result as we got earlier with $10 \times \frac{1}{4}$. $\frac{1}{4}$ **of** 10

        $$= \frac{1}{4} \times 10 = \frac{\cancel{10}^{5}}{\cancel{4}_{2}} = 2\frac{1}{2}.$$

    *   Use the same discs to illustrate interpret $\frac{3}{4}$ of 10.

        o   We found $\frac{1}{4}$ of $10 = \frac{10}{4} = 2\frac{1}{2}$. To find $\frac{3}{4}$ of 10 we can multiply that answer by 3.

        $$\frac{3}{4} \text{ of } 10 = 3 \times \frac{1}{4} \times 10 = 3 \times \frac{10}{4} = 7\frac{1}{2}.$$

        o   So $\frac{3}{4}$ of 10 is three of the equal groups, or $7\frac{1}{2}$.

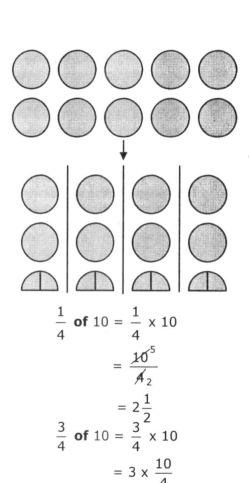

$$\frac{1}{4} \times 10 = \frac{\cancel{10}^{5}}{\cancel{4}_{2}}$$
$$= 2\frac{1}{2}$$

$$\frac{1}{4} \text{ of } 10 = \frac{1}{4} \times 10$$
$$= \frac{\cancel{10}^{5}}{\cancel{4}_{2}}$$
$$= 2\frac{1}{2}$$

$$\frac{3}{4} \text{ of } 10 = \frac{3}{4} \times 10$$
$$= 3 \times \frac{10}{4}$$

Copyright © 2005 SingaporeMath.com Inc., Oregon

- ○ If we divide each of the wholes in our 3 equal groups into fourths, we have a total of 30 fourths. So $\frac{3}{4} \times 10 = \frac{3 \times 10}{4} = \frac{30}{4}$, which simplifies to $7\frac{1}{2}$.

$$\frac{3}{4} \times 10 = \frac{3 \times 10}{4}$$
$$= \frac{30}{4}$$
$$= \frac{15}{2}$$
$$= 7\frac{1}{2}$$

- ○ Point out to students that to simplify $\frac{30}{4}$, we divided both the numerator and denominator by a common factor. (Since we are given factors before we multiply, we can simplify before multiplying.) We show this method of simplifying by crossing out the number in the numerator and the number in the denominator and writing the quotient. This process is called <u>cancellation</u>.

$$\frac{3}{4} \times 10 = \frac{3 \times 10}{4}$$
$$= \frac{3 \times \cancel{10}^{5}}{\cancel{4}_{2}}$$
$$= \frac{15}{2}$$
$$= 7\frac{1}{2}$$

- ○ Show students how we save written steps by showing the cancellation in the original expression.

$$\frac{3}{\cancel{4}_{2}} \times \cancel{10}^{5} = \frac{15}{2} = 7\frac{1}{2}$$

- Write and discuss another example which uses cancellation, such as the one show here.
  - ○ We can cancel in steps. We can first divide the numerator and denominator by 2, and then by 7.
  - ○ Tell students to always write in the result of the cancellation, even when the result is only 1. This prevents them from thinking that somehow the number just disappears. 14 didn't just go away; the fraction was simplified to a denominator of 1.

$$\frac{3}{14} \text{ of } 28 = \frac{3 \times 28}{14}$$
$$= \frac{3 \times \cancel{28}^{14}}{\cancel{14}_{7}}$$
$$= \frac{3 \times \cancel{28}^{\cancel{14}^{2}}}{\cancel{14}_{\cancel{7}_{1}}}$$
$$= \frac{3 \times 2}{1}$$
$$= 6$$

2. Discuss **p. 44** and **tasks 1-2, textbook p. 45**

3. Provide additional practice. You can use **problems 1-3, Practice 3D, textbook p. 48**.

Copyright © 2005 SingaporeMath.com Inc., Oregon

Activity 3.4b   **Convert fractional measurements**

1. Review conversion of measurements involving whole numbers.
    *   Ask the students to name various units of measure for length, weight, volume of liquid, and time. Use various measuring devices or discuss the distance to some place (for kilometer and mile) to help them visualize their relative magnitudes between

	US:
1 meter and 1 centimeter	1 yard and 1 foot
1 kilometer and 1 meter	1 foot and 1 inch
1 kilogram and 1 gram	1 pound and 1 ounce
1 liter and 1 milliliter	1 gallon and 1 quart
	1 quart and 1 cup

    *   Have students list the conversion factors. (See the table on **p. 46 of the textbook**).
    *   Have students convert some whole numbers of a larger unit into a smaller unit. They need to multiply by the conversion unit.

        4 min = 4 x 60 s = 240 s

    *   Have students convert some measurements in compound units to the smaller unit. They need to multiply the part that is in the larger measurement unit to a smaller unit by multiplying by the conversion factor, and then adding the remaining measure.

        4 min 30 s = 240 s + 30 s
                   = 270 s

    *   Have students convert some measurement in a smaller unit to a compound unit. They need to split the measurement into a multiple of the conversion factor and the remainder, or divide by the conversion factor to get a quotient and remainder.

        372 s = 6 min 12 s
        360 s   12 s

    *   For additional practice, you can use **problem 11** in **workbook review 1**, if you have saved this problem for this unit, or use problems such as:

2 m = _____ cm	2 m = 2 x 100 cm = 200 cm
7 kg = _____ g	7 kg = 7 x 1000 g = 7000 g
2 days = ____ hours	2 days = 2 x 24 hours = 48 hours
2 days = ____ minutes	2 days = 48 hours x 60 min = 2880 min
8 min = ____ s	8 min = 8 x 60 s = 480 s

        US:

3 gal = ____ qt	3 gal = 3 x 4 qt = 12 qt
2 days = ____ hours	2 days = 2 x 24 hours = 48 hours
4 ft = ____ in.	4 ft = 4 x 12 in. = 48 in.
8 min = ____ s	8 min = 8 x 60 s = 480 s

2. Discuss converting a fraction (less than 1 whole) of a unit to a smaller unit.
    *   Ask students for the number of months in half of a year. Write the multiplication equation on the board.
    *   Lead students to see that by finding the number of months in half a year, we are essentially cutting up the year into 12 months, and then finding half of those 12

    $$\frac{1}{2} \text{ year} = \frac{1}{2} \text{ of 12 months}$$
    $$= \frac{1}{2} \times 12 \text{ months}$$
    $$= 6 \text{ months}$$

Copyright © 2005 SingaporeMath.com Inc., Oregon

months. We can do this by multiplying the fraction of the year by the number of months in a year. You can illustrate this with a diagram.

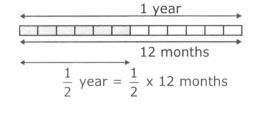

$$\frac{1}{2} \text{ year} = \frac{1}{2} \times 12 \text{ months}$$

- Have students find the number of months in a fourth of a year and in a sixth of a year by multiplying the fraction by the conversion factor (the number of months in a year).
- Ask students to find the number of months in $\frac{5}{6}$ of a year (**task 3, textbook p. 46**). They can to this mentally by multiplying the number of months in a sixth of a year by 5, or by writing and solving the equation.

$$\frac{1}{6} \text{ year} = \frac{1}{6} \times 12 \text{ months} = 2 \text{ months.}$$

$$\frac{5}{6} \text{ year} = 2 \text{ months} \times 5 = 10 \text{ months}$$

$$\frac{1}{6} \text{ year} = \frac{5}{\cancel{6}_1} \times \cancel{12}^{2} \text{ months} = 10 \text{ months}$$

3. Have students do **task 4, textbook p. 46**.

4. Discuss **task 5, textbook p. 46**.
   To convert a measurement expressed as a mixed number into compound units, we only need to convert the fractional part to the smaller unit.

$$\frac{3}{4} h = \frac{3}{4} \times 60 \text{ min} = 45 \text{ min}$$

$$2\frac{3}{4} h = 2 \text{ h } 45 \text{ min}$$

5. Have students do **task 6, textbook p. 46**.

Workbook Exercise 19

Activity 3.4c   **Convert fractional measurements**

1. Discuss converting a measurement given as a mixed number to a smaller unit.
   - Refer to **task 7, textbook p. 47**.
   - Lead students to see that we split up the mixed number into two parts, the whole number part and the fractional part. We then convert each part separately into the smaller unit. Then we combine the parts by adding.
   - Discuss **task 8, textbook p. 47**.

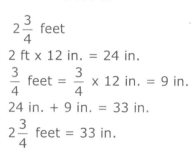

   - US: Have your student convert $2\frac{3}{4}$ feet into inches.

$$2\frac{3}{4} \text{ feet}$$
$$2 \text{ ft} \times 12 \text{ in.} = 24 \text{ in.}$$
$$\frac{3}{4} \text{ feet} = \frac{3}{4} \times 12 \text{ in.} = 9 \text{ in.}$$
$$24 \text{ in.} + 9 \text{ in.} = 33 \text{ in.}$$
$$2\frac{3}{4} \text{ feet} = 33 \text{ in.}$$

2. Have students do **task 9, textbook p. 47**.

3. Have students do **problems 4-9, Practice 3D, textbook p. 48**.

Workbook Exercise 20

Copyright © 2005 SingaporeMath.com Inc., Oregon

Activity 3.4d   **Fraction of a whole**

1. Discuss converting a measurement given as a whole number into a fraction or a mixed number of a larger unit.

    *   Ask student how we find a fraction of a whole. For example, say we have 12 counters. 4 are yellow and 8 are red. How do we find what fraction of the counters are yellow? 4 out of 12 counters are yellow. We put the part over the total number of counters.

4 yellow out of 12 total

$$\frac{4}{12} = \frac{1}{3}$$

$\frac{1}{3}$ of the counters are yellow.

    *   Tell students we have seen how to convert from a larger unit (year) into a smaller unit (months). What if we want to find what fraction of a year is 4 months? We want to find one number, 4 months, as a fraction of a whole amount, 1 year.
    *   To find 4 months as a fraction of a year we also put the part over the whole. But we have to use the same units. We need to find 4 months as a fraction of 12 months, which is a year.

4 months = what fraction of a year?

$$\frac{4}{12} = \frac{1}{3}$$

$\frac{1}{3}$ of the year is 4 months.

$$\frac{27}{12} = 2\frac{3}{12} = 2\frac{1}{4}$$

27 months is $2\frac{1}{4}$ years

    *   Ask students to find 27 months as a fraction of a year. We write it as the part over the total in the same size unit, or 12 months, since 1 year = 12 months. Then we simplify.
    *   Ask them to find 27 months as a fraction of 3 years. This time, 36 months is the whole, since 3 years = 3 x 12 months = 36 months.

$$\frac{27}{36} = \frac{3}{4}$$

27 months is $\frac{3}{4}$ of 3 years

(27 is $\frac{3}{4}$ of 36)

    *   US: Ask students to find 12 ounces as a fraction of 3 quarts. You can show 3 quart jars with one jar filled to 12 ounces, or draw them on the board and mark one as filled up to 12 ounces ($\frac{3}{4}$ of one of the jars).

3 qt = 3 x 16 oz = 48 oz

$$\frac{12}{48} = \frac{1}{4}$$

12 oz is $\frac{1}{4}$ of 3 qt.

2. Have students do **task 10, textbook p. 47**.

3. Have students do **problems 10-13, Practice 3D, textbook p. 48**.

Workbook Exercise 21

Copyright © 2005 SingaporeMath.com Inc., Oregon

| **Part 5: Product of Fractions** | **3 sessions** |

Objectives

- Multiply a fraction by a fraction.

Materials

- Index cards

Homework

- Workbook Exercise 22
- Workbook Exercise 23

Notes

In this section, students will learn to multiply a fraction by a fraction. Grids are used to give the students a concrete understanding of the procedure.

Students learned to interpret $\frac{1}{3}$ x 9 as $\frac{1}{3}$ of 9, or 3. We divide

the 9 into 3 equal groups. Likewise, $\frac{1}{3}$ x $\frac{1}{4}$ is $\frac{1}{3}$ of $\frac{1}{4}$. To

illustrate this, we usually draw a rectangle and cut it up in 2 directions. So we cut up the rectangle into fourths using vertical lines, and then draw horizontal lines to divide the rectangle (and each vertical line) into thirds. That is, we divide the rectangle into fourths, and then divide each fourth into thirds to

find one third of each fourth, so we see that $\frac{1}{3}$ of $\frac{1}{4}$ is $\frac{1}{12}$.

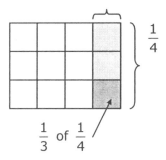

Likewise, we can see from such a drawing that $\frac{2}{3}$ of $\frac{3}{4}$ is $\frac{6}{12}$

or $\frac{1}{2}$. The total number of parts (12) is the product of the

denominators, 3 x 4. The number of parts we need (6) is the product of the numerators, 2 x 3. So answer is 2 x 3 parts out

of 3 x 4 parts, or $\frac{2\times3}{3\times4}$. After practicing several problems like

this, students will see that to multiply fractions, we multiply the

numerators and the denominators: $\frac{2}{3}\times\frac{3}{4}=\frac{2\times3}{3\times4}=\frac{6}{12}=\frac{1}{2}$

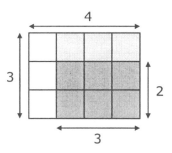

$$\frac{2}{3}\times\frac{3}{4}=\frac{2\times3}{3\times4}=\frac{6}{12}=\frac{1}{2}$$

Here, we multiplied and then simplified. Since to simplify we divide both the numerator and denominator by a common factor, it is easier to do the simplifying before multiplying, since

we already have some of the factors. $\frac{2}{3}\times\frac{3}{4}=\frac{2\times\cancel{3}^{1}}{\cancel{3}_{1}\times4}=\frac{\cancel{2}^{1}}{\cancel{4}_{2}}=\frac{1}{2}$, or $\frac{2}{3}\times\frac{3}{4}=\frac{\cancel{2}^{1}\times\cancel{3}^{1}}{\cancel{3}_{1}\times\cancel{4}_{2}}=\frac{1}{2}$. Or,

simply, $\frac{\cancel{2}^{1}}{\cancel{3}_{1}}\times\frac{\cancel{3}^{1}}{\cancel{4}_{2}}=\frac{1}{2}$.

Copyright © 2005 SingaporeMath.com Inc., Oregon

Activity 3.5a   **Product of fractions**

1. Illustrate finding a fraction of a fraction, using grid diagrams.
   - Have students do the activity on **p. 49 of the textbook**. They can use index cards.
   - Have students use rectangles to find some other some other simple fractions, such as:

   $$\frac{1}{2} \times \frac{2}{3} \qquad\qquad \frac{1}{4} \times \frac{3}{4} \qquad\qquad \frac{3}{4} \times \frac{4}{5}$$

   - Discuss their results.
   - Have students do **tasks 1-4, textbook p. 50-51**.

2. Discuss finding a fraction of a fraction as the product of the numerators over the product of the denominators.

   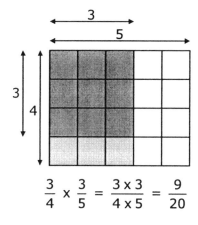

   $$\frac{3}{4} \times \frac{3}{5} = \frac{3 \times 3}{4 \times 5} = \frac{9}{20}$$

   - Draw a rectangle on the board and divide it in fifths with vertical lines. Shade $\frac{3}{5}$. Draw three lines horizontally to show fourths. Shade $\frac{3}{4}$ of $\frac{3}{5}$ with a darker color and write $\frac{3}{4} \times \frac{3}{5}$.
     - Ask students how they would find the total number of small rectangles there are now. Since there are 4 rows and 5 columns, the total number of small rectangles is 4 x 5 = 20. Each small rectangle is $\frac{1}{20}$ of the total.
     - Ask them how they would find the number of darker rectangles. There 3 rows and 3 columns, so there are 3 x 3 = 9 dark rectangles. The dark rectangles are $\frac{9}{20}$ of the whole.
     - So $\frac{3}{4} \times \frac{3}{5} = \frac{9}{20}$. Point out that the total number of rectangles is the same as the product of the denominators, while the number of dark rectangles is the product of the numerators. We can find $\frac{3}{4} \times \frac{3}{5}$ by multiplying the numerators together to find the number of parts, and multiplying the denominators together to find the total parts.
   - Use another drawing to show that $\frac{3}{5} \times \frac{3}{4} = \frac{3 \times 3}{5 \times 4}$.
   - Have students use this method (rather than counting squares) for **tasks 1-4, textbook pp. 50-51**.

   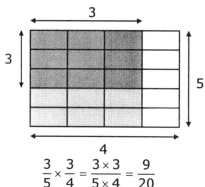

   $$\frac{3}{5} \times \frac{3}{4} = \frac{3 \times 3}{5 \times 4} = \frac{9}{20}$$

Copyright © 2005 SingaporeMath.com Inc., Oregon

Activity 3.5b

Product of fractions

1. Review finding a fraction of a fraction using multiplication.
   - Refer to **task 5, textbook p. 51**.
   - Remind students that a fraction times a fraction means that we are finding a fraction **of** a fraction, and we can do this by multiplying the numerators together to get the numerator of the answer, since this gives us the number of parts we want, and multiplying the denominators together to get the total number of parts. Have them illustrate this with a grid as before.

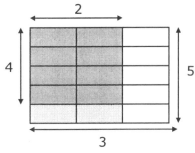

$$\frac{4}{5} \times \frac{2}{3} = \frac{4 \times 2}{5 \times 3} = \frac{8}{15}$$

2. Discuss simplifying before multiplying.

   - Illustrate $\frac{2}{3}$ of $\frac{3}{4}$ with a grid.

   - Point out that when we find the product, we can simplify it to $\frac{1}{2}$. To simplify it, we divided the numerator and denominator by 6. We could also have divided first by 3, and then by 2. These are common factors of the numerator and denominator.

   - Tell students it is often easier to simplify before multiplying, since we already have some of the factors. We can even show this with the original two fractions, as in $\dfrac{\cancel{2}^{\,1}}{\cancel{3}_{\,1}} \times \dfrac{\cancel{3}^{\,1}}{\cancel{4}_{\,2}} = \dfrac{1}{2}$.

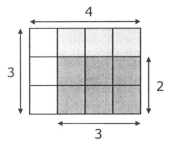

$$\frac{2}{3} \times \frac{3}{4} = \frac{2 \times 3}{3 \times 4} = \frac{6}{12} = \frac{1}{2}$$

$$\frac{2}{3} \times \frac{3}{4} = \frac{2 \times \cancel{3}^{\,1}}{\cancel{3}_{\,1} \times 4} = \frac{\cancel{2}^{\,1}}{\cancel{4}_{\,2}} = \frac{1}{2}$$

$$\text{or, } \frac{2}{3} \times \frac{3}{4} = \frac{\cancel{2}^{\,1} \times \cancel{3}^{\,1}}{\cancel{3}_{\,1} \times \cancel{4}_{\,2}} = \frac{1}{2}$$

$$\text{or, } \frac{\cancel{2}^{\,1}}{\cancel{3}_{\,1}} \times \frac{\cancel{3}^{\,1}}{\cancel{4}_{\,2}} = \frac{1}{2}$$

   - Discuss **task 6, textbook p. 51**.

      If we calculated the product before simplifying, we would have $\dfrac{45}{120}$ and would then divide both the numerator and denominator by 15 (or by 3 and also by 5). We can simplify before multiplying, as in method 1. We can show this with the original fractions, as in method 2. Since $\dfrac{9}{10} \times \dfrac{5}{12} = \dfrac{9 \times 5}{10 \times 12} = \dfrac{5 \times 9}{10 \times 12} = \dfrac{5}{10} \times \dfrac{9}{12} = \dfrac{1}{2} \times \dfrac{3}{4}$ we can simplify by dividing the 9 (of $\dfrac{9}{10}$) and the 12 (of $\dfrac{5}{12}$) by the common factor 3.

3. Have students do **task 7, textbook p. 51**.

Copyright © 2005 SingaporeMath.com Inc., Oregon

4. Discuss finding area when the lengths are fractions. The idea that multiplication leads to a smaller number is sometimes hard for students to grasp, particularly in finding area when fractions are used. In **task 3 on p. 50 of the textbook**, the area of a rectangle measuring $\frac{1}{3}$ m by $\frac{5}{6}$ m is found to be $\frac{5}{18}$ m². $\frac{5}{18}$ being smaller than the two factors may not have caused comment, since there was a drawing with this task. However, if you ask a student to find the area of a rectangle measuring $\frac{1}{2}$ m by $\frac{1}{2}$ m using $\frac{1}{2} \times \frac{1}{2} = \frac{1}{2 \times 2} = \frac{1}{4}$, a student may just look at the numbers and find it odd that the area seems to be smaller than each side. The following discussion may help with this concept.

- Write 2 x 2 and ask students to find the product.
  - ○ Point out that when multiplying two whole numbers together, the product is greater than each of the numbers by itself.

- Write $2 \times \frac{1}{2}$ and ask students to find the product.

  - ○ Point out that the product is larger than $\frac{1}{2}$, but smaller than 2. We are finding a fraction of the 2.

- Write $\frac{1}{2} \times \frac{1}{2}$ and ask students to find the product.

  - ○ Point out that the product is smaller than both the factors. We are finding a fraction of a fraction.

- Draw a square, label the side of the square as 1 m, and mark $\frac{1}{2}$ m on two adjacent sides. Make a square with these sides. Show that the area of the little square is $\frac{1}{4}$ of the area of the larger square. $\frac{1}{2}$ m x $\frac{1}{2}$ m = $\frac{1}{4}$ m². Although the fraction $\frac{1}{4}$ is smaller than the fraction $\frac{1}{2}$, they are not both a fraction of the same thing. $\frac{1}{4}$ is a fraction of a square meter, whereas the $\frac{1}{2}$ is a fraction of a meter length. The sides are a fraction of the total length of 1 m, and the area ($\frac{1}{4}$ m²) is a fraction of the square with an area of 1 m².

$2 \times 2 = 4$

$2 \times \frac{1}{2} = 1$

$\frac{1}{2} \times 2 = 1$

$\frac{1}{2} \times \frac{1}{2} = \frac{1}{4}$

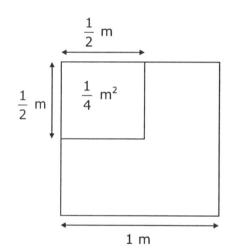

Workbook Exercise 22

Copyright © 2005 SingaporeMath.com Inc., Oregon

Activity 3.5c   **Practice and word problems**

1. Have students do **Practice 3E, textbook p. 52** and share their solutions.
   - If any of the word problems are confusing, guide them in drawing a picture (not necessarily a bar model). For example for problem 9, they could draw a cake, show about $\frac{1}{6}$ eaten, and then mark about $\frac{1}{5}$ of the remainder as the part given away. So we need to find $\frac{1}{5}$ of $\frac{5}{6}$.

2. Game

   Material for each group of about 4 players: 4 sets of number cards 1-9

   Procedure: Shuffle cards and deal them all out. Each player turns over four of their cards to form two fractions and multiplies the fractions together. The player with the highest product gets all the cards. They repeat with the next four cards. The player with the most cards at the end wins.

   After playing this game with multiplication, students can try it with addition. Since they are trying to get the highest sum, they may realize after a while that if they use the smaller two numbers as denominators, they will get a larger sum than if they use a larger number.

Copyright © 2005 SingaporeMath.com Inc., Oregon

Part 6: Dividing a Fraction by a Whole Number   2 sessions

Objectives

- Divide a fraction by a whole number.

Materials

- Index cards

Homework

- Workbook Exercise 24
- Workbook Exercise 25

Notes

In this section, students are introduced to the concept of dividing a fraction by a whole number.

$3 \div 4$ can be interpreted as $\frac{1}{4}$ of 3, or $\frac{3}{4}$. Similarly, $\frac{2}{3} \div 4$ can be interpreted as $\frac{1}{4}$ of $\frac{2}{3}$, or $\frac{1}{4} \times \frac{2}{3}$. Since $\frac{1}{4} \times \frac{2}{3} = \frac{2}{3} \times \frac{1}{4}$, we can say that $\frac{2}{3} \div 4 = \frac{2}{3} \times \frac{1}{4}$. Dividing by 4 is the same as multiplying by $\frac{1}{4}$. Students should understand this concept before they are taught to "invert and multiply".

Copyright © 2005 SingaporeMath.com Inc., Oregon

Activity 3.6a   **Divide a fraction by a whole number**

1. Illustrate division of a fraction by a whole number.

   - Discuss the example on **p. 53 of the textbook**. Students should see that $\frac{2}{3} \div 4$ is

     equivalent to $\frac{1}{4}$ of $\frac{2}{3}$, and that we can find the value of $\frac{2}{3} \div 4$ by changing $\div 4$ to $\times \frac{1}{4}$.

     That is, $\frac{2}{3} \div 4 = \frac{2}{3} \times \frac{1}{4}$.

   - Discuss **task 1, textbook p. 54**. Point out that the rectangle was divided into thirds by

     the vertical line, and $\frac{2}{3}$ was shaded to show $\frac{2}{3}$. Then the $\frac{2}{3}$ was divided by 3 using

     horizontal lines. You may want to show each step on the board. So $\frac{2}{3}$ divided by 3 is

     the same as $\frac{1}{3}$ of $\frac{2}{3}$, or $\frac{2}{3} \times \frac{1}{3}$

   - Provide another example.
     - Draw a rectangle on the board and divide it into
       fifths. Students can do the same thing with an

       index card. Shade $\frac{2}{5}$. Write the expression $\frac{2}{5} \div$

       4. Lead students to see that they can divide the

       $\frac{2}{5}$ into 4 equal parts by drawing horizontal lines.

       Shade one part to show $\frac{2}{5} \div 4$. This is the same

       as $\frac{1}{4}$ of $\frac{2}{5}$, or $\frac{2}{5} \times \frac{1}{4}$. The answer, $\frac{2}{20}$ simplifies

       to $\frac{1}{10}$.

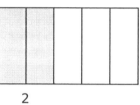

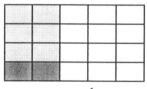

$$\frac{2}{5} \div 4 = \frac{\cancel{2}^{1}}{5} \times \frac{1}{\cancel{4}_{2}} = \frac{1}{10}$$

2. Divide a fraction by a whole number.
   - Discuss **task 2, textbook p. 54**.
   - Have students do **task 3, textbook p. 54**.

   Workbook Exercise 24

Activity 3.6b   **Word problems**

1. Have students do **Practice 3F, textbook p. 55** and share their solutions.
   - If any of the word problems are confusing, have them illustrate the problems. They can
     use bar models or other drawings. For example in problem 8 they can draw the square

     flower bed. If the perimeter is $\frac{3}{4}$ m, then they need to divide by 4 to find the length of a

     side.

   Workbook Exercise 25

Copyright © 2005 SingaporeMath.com Inc., Oregon

Part 7: Word Problems   **4 sessions**

Objectives

- Solve multi-step word problems involving fractions.

Materials

- Index cards

Homework

- Workbook Exercise 26
- Workbook Exercise 27
- Workbook Exercise 28
- Workbook Exercise 29

Notes

In *Primary Mathematics 4A*, students learned to use fraction bars to solve word problems involving fractions. Each fractional part of the bar is a unit, similar to the unit in the part-whole model for multiplication and division. For example, to find $\frac{2}{3}$ x 18, we can draw a bar and divide it into thirds, or 3 units. Knowing the value of 3 units (18) we can find the value of 1 unit and of 2 units.

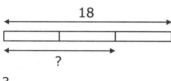

$\frac{3}{3}$ = 3 units = 18

$\frac{1}{3}$ = 1 unit = 18 ÷ 3 = 6

$\frac{2}{3}$ = 2 units = 6 x 2 = 12

The part-whole model was used to find the whole when given a fractional part. For example, if we know that $\frac{3}{5}$ of some number is 15, we can use the model to find the number. We can draw a bar, divide it into fifths, and label 3 units as 15. Then we see that we can find $\frac{1}{5}$, or 1 unit, by dividing by 3, and then find the total (5 units) by multiplying the value for 1 unit by 5.

$\frac{3}{5}$ = 3 units = 15

$\frac{1}{5}$ = 1 unit = 15 ÷ 3 = 5

$\frac{5}{5}$ = 5 units = 5 x 5 = 25

This kind of problem is essentially a fractional division problem; we need to find $\frac{3}{5}$ of what is 15, or 15 ÷ $\frac{3}{5}$. Students have not yet learned to divide by a fraction. Instead, they will solve these kinds of problems with a unitary approach; that is, by finding the value for 1 unit or for the unit fraction. Modeling the problem makes this easy to visualize.

In this section, they will learn to solve multi-step word problems involving fractions. Encourage students to draw models when needed.

Copyright © 2005 SingaporeMath.com Inc., Oregon

Activity 3.7a   **Word problems**

1. Discuss word problems involving finding a fractional part of a given whole.
   - Discuss the example on **p. 56 of the textbook**. Make sure students understand that we are given the fraction of money spent and need to find the amount saved. Three methods are shown.
     - Method 1 involves first finding the fraction that she saved, and using that to find the dollar amount of the total.
     - Method 2 involves first finding the dollar amount spent, and then subtracting that from the total to find the amount saved.
     - Method 3 involves a part-whole model. Ask students why the bar is divided into 5 units. (Each unit represents a fifth.) Ask them what the shaded part represents (the amount spent) and what the unshaded part represents (the amount saved). We know the total amount, and can label that on the bar. The first step in solving the problem is to find the value for 1 unit, which is the value for $\frac{1}{5}$ of the total. Once the value of $\frac{1}{5}$ is found, then the value of any number of fifths can easily be found. Point out to students that when using this method, we generally try to find the value of one unit first, as we did with problems involving whole numbers.
   - Discuss **task 1, textbook p. 57**. You can discuss each of the three methods:
     - Method 1:

       Fraction of boys = $1 - \frac{5}{8} = \frac{3}{8}$

       Number of boys = $\frac{3}{8}$ x 96 = 3 x 12 = 36
     - Method 2:

       Number of girls = $\frac{5}{8}$ x 96 = 60

       Number of boys = 96 – 60 = 36
     - Method 3:

       8 units = 96
       1 unit = 96 ÷ 8 = 12
       3 units = 12 x 3 = 36 boys
   - Discuss **task 2, textbook p. 57**. You can discuss several methods:
     - We can first draw a bar with 5 units. Each unit is $\frac{1}{5}$. Then we can divide each unit in half to show tenths. Or, we can realize ahead of time that we will need like fractions.

       David spent $\frac{1}{5} = \frac{2}{10}$ of his money on a storybook.

       10 units = $40
       1 unit = $40 ÷ 10 = $4
       5 units = $4 x 5 = $20
       Or: 5 is half of 10 units, or the total. Half of $40 is $20.
     - Fraction spent = $\frac{1}{5} + \frac{3}{10} = \frac{2}{10} + \frac{3}{10} = \frac{5}{10} = \frac{1}{2}$

       Amount he spent = $\frac{1}{2}$ x $40 = $20

Copyright © 2005 SingaporeMath.com Inc., Oregon

- Provide a problem for students to model. For example:
  - ➤ Mary had \$350. She spent $\frac{4}{7}$ of it. How much money did she have left? (\$150)

2. Discuss word problems involving finding the whole when given the value of a fractional part.
   - Discuss **task 3, textbook p. 57**.
     - ○ Ask students to relate the drawing to the information in the problem. For example, ask them what the shaded units represent. The shaded 5 units represent 300 eggs.
     - ○ Guide them in finding how many eggs one unit represents, and then how many are represented by 8 units, or the whole.

5 units = 300	Or: $\frac{5}{8}$ of total = 300
1 unit = 300 ÷ 5 = 60	$\frac{1}{8}$ of total = $\frac{300}{5}$ = 60
8 units = 60 x 8 = 480	$\frac{8}{8}$ of total = 60 x 8 = 480

Workbook Exercise 64

Activity 3.7b   **More word problems**

1. Continue to discuss word problems involving finding the whole when given the value of a fractional part.
   - Have students share their solutions for **workbook exercise 64**.
   - Provide other problems for students to solve. Have them share their drawings. For example:
     - ➤ After spending $\frac{5}{11}$ of her money, Sue had \$36 left. How much did she spend? (\$30)
     - ➤ $\frac{3}{5}$ of the guests at a party were girls. There were 3 fewer boys at the party than girls. How many boys and girls were at the party? (Since there are $\frac{1}{5}$ fewer boys than girls, $\frac{1}{5}$ of the number of children = 3 and the total number is 3 x 5 = 15.)
     - ➤ A pet shop sold $\frac{1}{3}$ of its puppies in the first week and $\frac{1}{4}$ of the puppies the second week. If it sold 14 puppies in those two weeks, how many puppies did it have at first? (24).
   - Students can do **problems 1, 2, and 4, Practice 3G, textbook p. 60**. A possible model for Problem 4 is shown here:

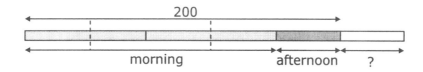

Copyright © 2005 SingaporeMath.com Inc., Oregon

2. Have students create word problems from drawings.
   - Provide students with some drawings and have them create fraction word problems that would be modeled as in the drawing. Let them see how creative they can be. For example:

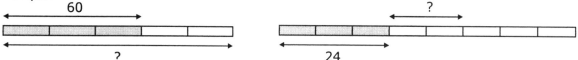

Workbook Exercise 27

Activity 3.7c   **Find the fraction of a remainder**

1. Discuss **task 4, textbook p. 58**.
   - It is probably easier to first discuss the method 2, which uses a diagram. Have students relate the diagram to the information in the written problem. The bar is divided up into 3 parts to represent thirds and one third is shaded to represent the number of stamps sold on Monday. The unshaded part is the remainder. Because we know the value of 3 parts, we can find the value of 2 parts, which is the remainder.

     3 units = 360
     1 unit = 360 ÷ 3 = 120
     2 units = 120 x 2 = 240

     The second bar shows that remainder, now divided into four units to represent fourths. Because we know the total value of the remainder (these 4 units) from the first step, we can find the value of 1 unit, which is the number of stamps he sold on Tuesday

     4 units = 240
     1 unit = 240 ÷ 4 = 60

   - Discuss the first method. In it, equations with fractions rather than units are used.
   - Discuss 2 other methods:
     ➢ Find the number of stamps sold on Monday:

     $$\frac{1}{3} \times 360 = 120$$

     Find the remainder:
         360 – 120 = 240
     Find the number sold on Tuesday:

     $$\frac{1}{4} \times 240 = 60$$

     ➢ Draw a bar showing thirds. See that dividing the remainder into fourths involves dividing that part in half, so we divide all the parts in half. There are now 6 units. 1 unit represents the number of stamps he sold on Tuesday.

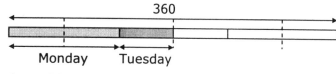

     6 units = 360
     1 unit = 360 ÷ 6 = 60

Copyright © 2005 SingaporeMath.com Inc., Oregon

2. Discuss **tasks 5-6, textbook p. 59**. There are at least 4 methods that can be used to solve each of these.
   - Task 5.
     1. Use the diagram in the text. First find the number unsold. Since she sold $\frac{3}{4}$, divide the bar into fourths. The amount unsold is one part.
        4 parts = 300
        1 part = 300 ÷ 4 = 75
        She had 75 unsold. Use this as the total for another bar for the remainder. Since she gave $\frac{1}{3}$ to the remainder, divide the second bar into thirds. The amount she has left is two of these units.
        3 units = 75
        1 unit = 75 ÷ 3 = 25
        2 units = 25 x 2 = 50

     2. Draw a bar for the total amount of tarts, and then divide into fourths, as before. Then further divide the last fourth into thirds, since she gave $\frac{1}{3}$ of one part to her neighbor. We can divide each of the other parts into thirds as well, so that we now have 12 units.

        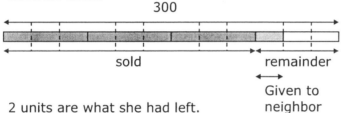

        2 units are what she had left.
        12 units = 300
        1 unit = 300 ÷ 12 = 25
        2 units = 25 x 2 = 50

     3. Remainder $= 1 - \frac{3}{4} = \frac{1}{4}$

        Amount remaining $= \frac{1}{4}$ x 300 = 75

        Fraction of remainder left $= 1 - \frac{1}{3} = \frac{2}{3}$

        Number of tarts left $= \frac{2}{3}$ x 75 = 2 x 25 = 50

     4. Number sold $= \frac{3}{4}$ x 300 = 225

        Remainder = 300 – 225 = 75

        Number given to neighbor $= \frac{1}{3}$ x 75 = 25

        Number of tarts left = 75 – 25 = 50

Copyright © 2005 SingaporeMath.com Inc., Oregon

- Task 6

    1. Use the diagram in the text. This shows that $\frac{1}{2}$ of the remainder ($\frac{3}{5}$) is $300.

        Remainder = $300 x 2 = $600
        He gave away 2 units, and had 3 units left, which is $600. His total is 5 units.
        3 units = $600
        1 unit = $600 ÷ 3 = $200
        5 units = $200 x 5 = $1000
        He had $1000 at first.

    2. We can use one bar with 5 equal parts, each representing $\frac{1}{5}$ of his money. Since he

        had $\frac{1}{2}$ of 3 parts left, we can cut three parts in half. Half of the remainder is one and

        a half parts. If we cut all the parts into half, we have 10 equal units.

        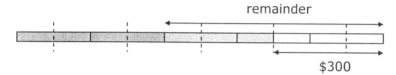

        The amount spent is 3 units, and he had 10 units total at first.
        3 units = $300
         1 unit = $300 ÷ 3 = $100
        10 units = $100 x 10 = $1000

    3. $\frac{1}{2}$ of the remainder = $300. All of the remainder = 2 x $300 = $600

        Fraction of total remaining = $1 - \frac{2}{5} = \frac{3}{5}$

        $\frac{3}{5}$ of his money = $600

        $\frac{1}{5}$ of his money = $600 ÷ 3 = $200

        $\frac{5}{5}$ of his money = $200 x 5 = $1000

    4. Fraction remaining: $1 - \frac{2}{5} = \frac{3}{5}$. $\frac{1}{2}$ of the remainder is left. $\frac{1}{2} \times \frac{3}{5} = \frac{3}{10}$

        $\frac{3}{10}$ of his money = $300

        $\frac{1}{10}$ of his money = $300 ÷ 3 = $100

        $\frac{10}{10}$ of his money = $100 x 10 = $1000

Workbook Exercise 28

Copyright © 2005 SingaporeMath.com Inc., Oregon

Activity 3.7d   **Practice**

1. Have students do the problems **in Practice 3G, textbook p. 60**, and share their methods. Possible methods are shown here for problems 3, 6, and 8

3.

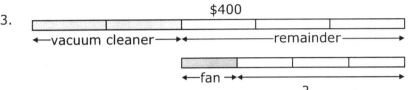

$400

←vacuum cleaner→ ←————remainder————→

←fan→ ←————?————→

Total = 5 parts = $400
1 part = $400 ÷ 5 = $80
Amount left after buying vacuum cleaner:
3 parts = $80 x 3 = $240
Divide remainder into 4 units.
Amount left is 3 units.
4 units = $240
1 unit = $240 ÷ 4 = $60
3 units = $60 x 3 = $180
He had $180 left.

Or:

The remainder was $\frac{3}{5}$ of his money.

After buying the fan, he had $\frac{3}{4}$ of the remainder left.

$\frac{3}{4}$ x $\frac{3}{5}$ x $400 = $180

6.

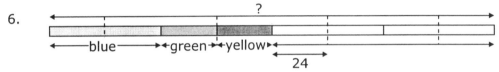

←——blue——→ ←green→ ←yellow→

24

Divide a bar into fourths, mark $\frac{1}{4}$ for blue marbles. Since $\frac{1}{8}$ were green, divide each fourth into half for eighths, mark $\frac{1}{8}$ for green marbles. The remainder is 5 units (eighths), so mark 1 unit (one fifth of remainder) for yellow marbles.
There is a total of 8 units.
1 unit = 24.
8 units = 24 x 8 = 192
He bought 192 marbles.

Or:

Remainder = $1 - \frac{1}{4} - \frac{1}{8} = 1 - \frac{2}{8} - \frac{1}{8} = \frac{5}{8}$

Fraction of marbles that are yellow:

$\frac{1}{5}$ x $\frac{5}{8}$ = $\frac{1}{8}$

$\frac{1}{8}$ of the marbles = 24

All of the marbles = 24 x 8 = 192

8.

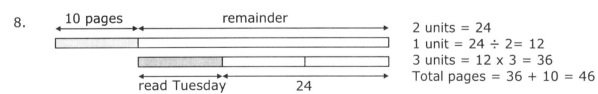

10 pages   remainder

read Tuesday   24

2 units = 24
1 unit = 24 ÷ 2 = 12
3 units = 12 x 3 = 36
Total pages = 36 + 10 = 46

2. Provide some drawings and have students make up problems that could be solved using the drawings.

Workbook Exercise 29

Copyright © 2005 SingaporeMath.com Inc., Oregon

Review

Objectives

- Review all topics.

Suggested number of sessions: 2

	Objectives	Textbook	Workbook	Activities
Review A				**2 sessions**
25	▪ Review.	pp. 61-64, Review A		R.1
26				

Activity R.1   **Review**

1. Select some of the problems in **Review A, textbook pp. 61-64** to work on as a class and have students work on others individually. You can also use some of this review as a source of problems for daily review as you cover the next units. Possible solutions for problems 40, 41, and 42 are shown here.

40. (a) Fraction left $= \dfrac{3}{5} \times \dfrac{2}{3} = \dfrac{6}{15} = \dfrac{2}{5}$

   (b) 3 smaller units = $600
        1 smaller unit = $200
        5 smaller units = $1000 = 2 larger units
        1 larger unit = $500
        3 larger units = $1500
        His salary is $1500.

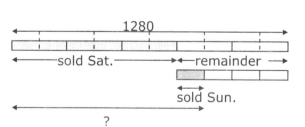

41.

$$6 - 1\frac{3}{4} - \left(3 \times \frac{3}{4}\right) = 5 - \frac{3}{4} - \frac{9}{4} = 5 - \frac{3}{4} - 2\frac{1}{4} = 4\frac{1}{4} - 2\frac{1}{4} = 2$$

   She had 2 m left.

42. 10 units = 1280
     1 unit = 1280 ÷ 10 = 128
     7 units = 7 x 128 = 896
     He sold 896 eggs on the two days.

Copyright © 2005 SingaporeMath.com Inc., Oregon

Unit 4 – Area of Triangle

Objectives

- Understand the formula for finding the area of a triangle.
- Find the area of triangles.
- Solve problems involving the area of a triangle.

Suggested number of sessions: 5

	Objectives	Textbook	Workbook	Activities
Part 1 : Finding the Area of a Triangle				**5 sessions**
49	▪ Review area. ▪ Find the area of a triangle using square grid paper.	pp. 65-66		4.1a
50	▪ Derive the formula for the area of a triangle. ▪ Find corresponding heights for different bases of a triangle.	p. 67, task 1	Ex. 30	4.1b
51	▪ Find the area of a triangle using a formula.	p. 68, tasks 2-3	Ex. 31-32	4.1c
52	▪ Solve problems involving area of a triangle and area of a rectangle.	p. 69, tasks 4-5	Ex. 33	4.1d
53	▪ Practice.	p. 70, Practice 4A		4.1e

Copyright © 2005 SingaporeMath.com Inc., Oregon

Copyright © 2005 SingaporeMath.com Inc., Oregon

| **Part 1: Finding the Area of a Triangle** | **5 sessions** |

Objectives

- Understand the formula for finding the area of a triangle.
- Find the area of triangles.
- Solve problems involving the area of a triangle.

Materials

- Centimeter graph paper or other square grid paper.

Homework

- Workbook Exercise 30
- Workbook Exercise 31
- Workbook Exercise 32
- Workbook Exercise 33

Notes

Students learned to find the area of a rectangle in *Primary Mathematics 3B,* given its length and width. This was reviewed in *Primary Mathematics 4A* and extended to finding one dimension when given the other dimension and either the area or the perimeter. Students also learned to find the area of composite figures made up of squares and rectangles.

This unit introduces the concept that the area of a triangle is half the area of a related rectangle. From this we can derive the formula:

$$\text{Area of a triangle} = \frac{1}{2} \times \text{base} \times \text{height}$$

where base and height are the sides of the related rectangle and are perpendicular to each other.

Initially, the triangles are drawn with the base horizontal (parallel to the bottom of the paper) so that the height is vertical. However, any side of the triangle can be considered the base.

Triangles can be grouped into three types according to their angles. Right triangles have one right angle. Acute triangles have all angles less than 90°. Obtuse triangles have one angle greater than 90°. For *Primary Mathematics*, the terms <u>acute</u> and <u>obtuse</u> do not need to be taught to students at this time. However, if your standards require your students to know these terms, you can teach them at this time.

Note: Activity 4.1a may be too long to do in one lesson. You can split it up and do part of it with activity 4.1b.

Copyright © 2005 SingaporeMath.com Inc., Oregon

Activity 4.1a   **Find area of triangles**

1. Review area and finding the area of composite figures.
    *   Remind students that the area of a figure is the amount of flat, two dimensional space it covers. Area is measured in square units. If the area of the figure is 4 square centimeters, then it covers the same amount of space as four squares each of whose sides is 1 centimeter.
    *   Draw a rectangle and label the lengths of the sides. Ask students for the area. They should remember that they can find the area of a rectangle by multiplying the lengths of the sides together.
    *   Draw a composite figure made up of rectangles and squares and ask students to find its area.
        *   We can find the area by splitting up the figure into rectangles, finding the area of each rectangle, and adding.
        *   We can also find the area by finding the area of the larger rectangle (25 cm x 15 cm) and subtracting the area of the two non-shaded rectangles (10 cm x 10 cm and 5 cm x 10 cm)
    *   Have students do **problems 15-18** and **22** in the **workbook Review 1**.
    *   You can also have students do **problems 22 and 23** on **p. 91** or **problem 12, p. 94** in the **textbook**.

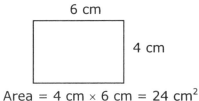

6 cm

4 cm

Area = 4 cm × 6 cm = 24 cm²

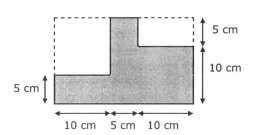

5 cm

10 cm

5 cm

10 cm   5 cm   10 cm

2. Find the area of triangles using square grid paper.
    *   Provide students with square grid paper.
    *   Have students mark a 6 by 6 square and have them draw a line from one corner to the opposite one to create a triangle. Have them find the area of this triangle by counting the squares. Lead them to see that the area of the triangle is half the area of the square.

    Area of square = 6 x 6 = 36 square units

    Area of triangle = $\frac{1}{2}$ x 36 = 18 square units

    *   Repeat with a triangle that is half of a 5 by 6 rectangle. Lead students to see that the area of the triangle is again half the area of the rectangle.

    Area of rectangle = 6 x 5 = 30 square units

    Area of triangle = $\frac{1}{2}$ x 30 = 15 square units

    *   Draw an acute triangle (a triangle with all angles less than 90°) on the board and the related rectangle. Label the lengths of the sides of the rectangle.

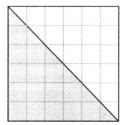

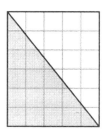

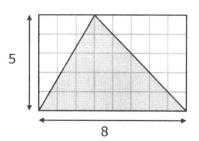

5

8

- Have students draw a similar figure with the same dimensions on square graph paper and ask them to find its area. See if they can come up with several methods:

  ➢ Count the squares.

  ➢ Cut out the rectangle and the unshaded parts. Rotate the unshaded parts to show that the areas of the unshaded part of the rectangle match the area of the triangle. The area of the triangle is half the area of the rectangle.

  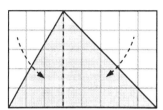

  ➢ (This method is less obvious.) Cut out the triangle and cut it into three pieces as shown and rearrange into a rectangle that is half the original related rectangle. The area of the triangle is half the area of the rectangle.

  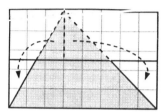

  ➢ Divide the triangle into two separate right triangles Find the areas of each right triangle by finding half the area of the rectangles, and add.

  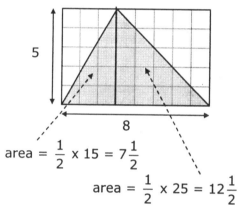

  $$\text{area} = \frac{1}{2} \times 15 = 7\frac{1}{2}$$

  $$\text{area} = \frac{1}{2} \times 25 = 12\frac{1}{2}$$

  $$\text{Total area} = 7\frac{1}{2} + 12\frac{1}{2} = 20 \text{ square units}$$

  ➢ Subtract the area of the two unshaded triangles from the area of the rectangle. This area is half the area of the rectangle.

  $$\text{area} = \frac{1}{2} \times 15 = 7\frac{1}{2}$$

  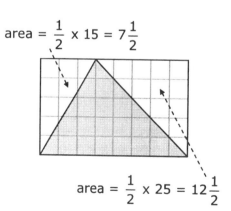

- Point out that the area of this kind of triangle is half the area of its related rectangle.

  $$\text{area} = \frac{1}{2} \times 25 = 12\frac{1}{2}$$

  $$\text{area of rectangle} = 8 \times 5 = 40 \text{ square units}$$

  $$\text{area of triangle} = 40 - 7\frac{1}{2} - 12\frac{1}{2} = 20 \text{ square units}$$

Copyright © 2005 SingaporeMath.com Inc., Oregon

- Draw an obtuse triangle with a base of 6 units and a height of 6 units on square grid paper and have students copy it.

- Have students find its area using several methods.

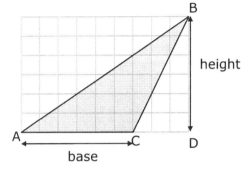

  ➢ Count the squares.

  ➢ Find the area of the larger right triangle (triangle ABD) and subtract the area of the smaller right triangle (triangle CBD) to get the area of the shaded triangle (triangle ABC). They find the area of the right triangles by finding the half the areas of the related rectangles.

Area of triangle ABD = $\frac{1}{2}$ x 54 = 27 square units

Area of triangle CBD = $\frac{1}{2}$ x 3 x 6 = 9 square units

Area of triangle ABC = 27 – 9 = 18 square units

  ➢ Show students how the triangle can be cut into three triangular pieces and rearranged to form a rectangle that is half of a rectangle. The width of the rectangle is the same as the length of one side of the triangle, and the height is even with the opposite vertex (the perpendicular distance to it). There are two ways that the pieces can be moved.
    ○ Slide piece X over so that C is at A, rotate and slide piece Y so that B ends up at A
    ○ Rotate and slide piece X to fit in next to piece Y and point C is at point B, then rotate and slice pieces X and Y together so they fit into the bottom half of the target rectangle next to piece Z.

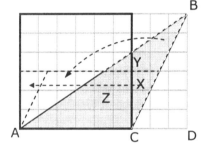

- Have students find the area of the related rectangle (6 x 6). Point out that the area of the triangle found by all of these methods is half of the area of this rectangle.

- Discuss each triangle on **pp. 65-66 in the textbook**. These triangles have different dimensions than the ones in this activity so far, but the area is still half the related rectangle.

Copyright © 2005 SingaporeMath.com Inc., Oregon

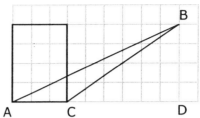

- Show your students one more triangle, an obtuse one which "leans over" farther. Guide them in finding the width, length, and area of the related rectangle. The width is the same as one side of the triangle and the length is the same as the perpendicular distance to the opposite vertex. For this triangle, it is harder to see how it can be cut up to fit into half the rectangle. But they can still show that the area of the triangle is half the area of the related rectangle by finding the area of right triangles ABD and CBD.

Area of triangle ABD = $\frac{1}{2}$ x 9 x 4 = 18 square units

Area of triangle CBD = $\frac{1}{2}$ x 6 x 4 = 12 square units

Area of triangle ABC = 18 – 12 = 6 square units

Area of triangle ABC = $\frac{1}{2}$ x base x height

$\qquad\qquad\qquad = \frac{1}{2}$ x 3 x 4 = 6 square units

- Have students draw other triangles on square grid paper, find a base and height, draw the related rectangles, find the area of the related rectangles, and the area of the triangles. They can see that the area of each triangle is half that of the related rectangle.

Activity 4.1b

Base, height, and formula for area of triangles

1. Discuss the formula for the area of a triangle.
   - Draw a right triangle and its related rectangle and label the base and height.
   - Tell students that we found that the area of the triangle was half the area of the rectangle. One side of the rectangle is the same as one side of the triangle, which we will call the base. The other side of the rectangle is the same as the distance to the vertex opposite the base. In a right triangle, this is perpendicular to the base.
   - Draw an acute triangle and label its base and height. The height is the perpendicular distance from the base to the opposite vertex. We found that the area of this triangle was half the area of a rectangle with the same dimensions as the triangle's base and height.
   - Draw an obtuse triangle and label its height and base. The height is again the perpendicular distance from the base to the opposite vertex. We found that the area for this triangle was half the area of a rectangle with the same base and height. You can have students find the area again as review. (It may help to have them refer again to the obtuse triangle on textbook p. 66.)

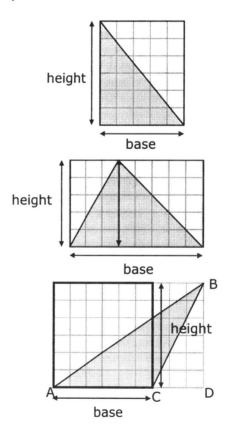

Copyright © 2005 SingaporeMath.com Inc., Oregon

- Summarize by writing the general formula for the area of any triangle on the board.

Area of triangle = $\frac{1}{2}$ x base x height

2. Have students find the area of the triangles in **task 1, textbook p. 67** using the formula for the area of a triangle.

3. Discuss base and height of triangles.
   - Tell students that any side can be used as a base for the triangle.
   - Draw an acute triangle with sides that are not parallel to the sides of the paper.
   - Show students different heights by using each of the 3 sides as a base. You can call on students to come up and draw the height. (They can use a ruler to draw the perpendicular line by laying the width of the ruler against the base and then sliding it along until the side touches the opposite vertex.)

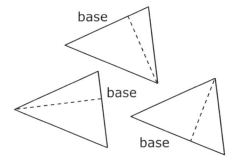

   - Repeat with an obtuse triangle. Note that for two of the sides, the base needs to be extended to enable drawing the corresponding heights.

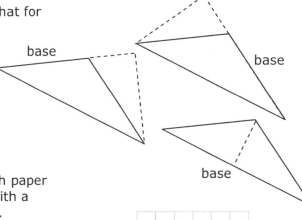

   - Provide students with centimeter graph paper and have them draw a right triangle with a base of 4 units and a height of 3 units.
     - Have them measure the third side (5 cm), draw a height from the third side, and measure it (about 2.4 cm).
     - Have them find the area using a different base and height each time. They should get the same area.

Workbook Exercise 30

Copyright © 2005 SingaporeMath.com Inc., Oregon

Activity 4.1c   **Find the area of triangles**

1. Review the formula for the area of a triangle and the base and height of a triangle.
   - Refer to **task 1.(a), textbook p. 67**.
     - Tell students we could say that the 8 cm side is the base. Have them turn their papers so that that side is parallel with the bottom edge of their desk. Ask them for the height. It would be the 6 cm side. Ask them to find the area with this new base and height. It is the same as if we used 6 cm as the base.
     - Point out that since multiplication can be done in any order, we do not have to first multiply the base and height together and then find half of that. We could find half of 6 first, and multiply that by 8, or half of 8 first, and multiply that by 6.
   - Refer to **task 1.(b), textbook p. 67**.
     - Tell students that we could use the longest side as the base, but then we don't know the length of the base and the height. When finding the area of a triangle, we pick a base whose length we know and where we can find the related height with the information given in the problem.

2. Discuss the fact that triangles with the same base and height have the same area.
   - Provide students with square graph paper.
   - Have students draw at least three triangles with the same base and height. You can show them an example on the board but encourage students to use a different base or height than you used, or draw yours on plain background but have them use square grid paper. Ask students to find the area of each triangle, using any method.
   - They should realize that since they all have the same base and height they will all have the same area, even though their shape differs. Write the formula for the area of a triangle on the board.

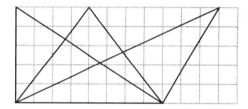

Area of triangle = $\frac{1}{2}$ x base x height

3. Use the formula for area of a triangle.
   - Have students do **task 2, textbook p. 68**.
   - After students have done these problems, remind them that multiplication can be done in any order. Ask them where this can help with their computations. For example, in 1.(c), $\frac{1}{2}$ x 10 x 12, it might be easier to find half of 12 rather than half of 10 first.

   When one of the sides is an odd number, as in 2(b), $\frac{1}{2}$ x 9 x 12, it is easier to first find half of the even number.

Workbook Exercises 31-32

Copyright © 2005 SingaporeMath.com Inc., Oregon

Activity 4.1d   **Triangle problem solving**

1. Have students work individually or in groups on **tasks 3-5, textbook pp. 68-69** and then share their solutions. Possible solutions for these are:
   - Task 3: Students need to be careful to pick an appropriate base and height. More measurements are given than needed to find the area. Remind them that the little square box at the intersection of two lines indicates that the two lines are perpendicular. In 3.(d) the base is 6 cm, and the height is 5 cm. If students have trouble seeing this, have them rotate their texts so that the 6 cm side is parallel to the bottom edge of their desks.
   - Task 4: This task is tricky. Students should use the rectangle to find the height of each triangle. In 4.(b), the 4 m side can be taken as the base, so the 18 m side would be the height. Again, if students have trouble seeing this, they can rotate their texts.
   - Task 5: Students should see that they need to subtract the area of the unshaded triangles from the area of the rectangles to find the area of the shaded part.

Workbook Exercise 33

Activity 4.1e   **Practice**

1. Have students work individually or in groups on the problems in **Practice 4A, textbook p. 70** and then share their solutions. Problem 4 is tricky. Possible solutions for 2-4:

   2. Base = 60 - 20 - 15 = 25 cm   Height = 12 cm

      Area = $\frac{1}{2}$ x 25 x 12 = 150 cm^2

   3. Area of each Δ = $\frac{1}{2}$ x 6 x 6 = 18 cm^2

      Area of figure = 8 x 18 = 144 cm^2

   4. (a) Students might try to find the area of each of the two obtuse triangles, on each side of the dotted vertical line; however, although both of them have a base of 7 cm, they can't find the individual heights. Some students might have an intuitive

      understanding of the distributive property and can find the area as $\frac{1}{2}$ x 7 x 18.

      Otherwise they will have to find the area of the large triangle formed by a base of 18 cm and a height of 5 + 7 = 12 cm and subtract the area of the small triangle with a base of 18 cm and a height of 5 cm to get the area of the shaded figure.

      Area = ($\frac{1}{2}$ x 18 x 12) - ($\frac{1}{2}$ x 18 x 5) = 108 - 45 = 63 cm^2.

   (b) Area = area of top triangle + area of bottom triangle

      = ($\frac{1}{2}$ x 110 x 40) + ($\frac{1}{2}$ x 66 x 88) = 2200 + 2904 = 5104 m^2

Copyright © 2005 SingaporeMath.com Inc., Oregon

Unit 5 – Ratio

Objectives

- Compare quantities expressed in the same unit using ratio.
- Find equivalent ratios.
- Express a ratio in simplest form.
- Interpret ratios in terms of units.
- Solve word problems involving ratio.

Suggested number of sessions: 7

	Objectives	Textbook	Workbook	Activities
Part 1 : Finding Ratio				**1 session**
54	▪ Compare two quantities using ratio. ▪ Interpret a given ratio in terms of units.	p. 71 pp. 72-74, tasks 1-9	Ex. 34	5.1a
Part 2 : Equivalent Ratios				**3 sessions**
55	▪ Find equivalent ratios. ▪ Express a ratio of two quantities in simplest form. ▪ Review common factors.	p. 75 p. 76, tasks 1-3	Ex. 34	5.2a
56	▪ Use the comparison model to represent a ratio of two quantities. ▪ Solve word problems involving ratios of two quantities.	pp. 77-78, tasks 4-6	Ex. 36	5.2b
57	▪ Practice.	p. 79, Practice 5A		5.2c
Part 3 : Comparing Three Quantities				**3 sessions**
58	▪ Compare three quantities using ratios. ▪ Write a given ratio of three quantities in simplest form.	p. 80 p. 81, task 1	Ex. 37	5.3a
59	▪ Solve word problems involving ratios of three quantities.	p. 81, task 2	Ex. 38	5.3b
60	▪ Practice.	p. 82, Practice 5B		5.3c

Copyright © 2005 SingaporeMath.com Inc., Oregon

Part 1: Finding Ratio	1 session

Objectives

* Compare two quantities expressed in the same unit using ratio.
* Interpret a ratio in terms of unit in a diagram.

Materials

* Counters or other objects, 2 colors

Homework

* Workbook Exercise 34

Notes

Students have learned how to compare two quantities by finding their difference and by finding how many times more one quantity is than another. In this section they will learn to compare two quantities by finding their ratio. In a ratio, the relative sizes of two or more quantities are being compared. For example, if one set has 3 oranges and the other set has 2 apples, the ratio of oranges to apples is 3 : 2. We read 3 : 2 as **3 to 2**. The ratio of oranges to total fruit is 3 : 5.

We can also compare two measurements. The measurements must always be in the same unit. To find the ratio of a length of 25 centimeters to 1 meter, we need to find the ratio of centimeters to centimeters or meters to meters. The ratio of the lengths is 25 : 100 (or 1 : 4). When expressing the ratio, we don't include the units, but we know that the units must be the same.

In a ratio, the first and second numbers represent the first and second quantities respectively. This order matters. In the example above, the ratio of oranges to apples is 3 : 2, but the ratio of apples to oranges is 2 : 3.

We use ratio to compare equal groups of differing quantities. For example, if we have 6 of one object, such as yellow counters, and 10 of another, such as red counters, we can group them by twos, and say we have 3 groups of yellow counters to 5 groups of red counters. We can also represent the equal groups as equal bar units.

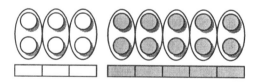

A given ratio does not indicate the actual size of the quantities involved, just their relative sizes. The ratio 3 : 5 in the example above tells us there are 3 yellow counters for every 5 red counters, but ratio does not tell us the actual number of each type of counter.

Copyright © 2005 SingaporeMath.com Inc., Oregon

Activity 5.1a   **Ratios**

1. Introduce ratios.
   - Discuss **p. 71** in the **textbook**.
   - Tell students that we can compare amounts using **ratios**.
   - Discuss other situations involving ratios, such as the ratio of the number of boys to girls in a class, or the number of students who wear glasses to students who don't.
   - Discuss **task 1, textbook p. 72**.
   - Point out that the ratio of white paint to red paint is different from the ratio of red paint to white paint.

2. Discuss using ratios to compare equal groups.
   - Display 6 counters of one color (such as yellow) and 10 of another color (such as red). (Or draw pictures of triangles and circles or other objects.) Put the counters into groups of 2. Each group is 1 unit.
   - Draw unit bars to represent the groups. Tell students that the value of each unit is the same.

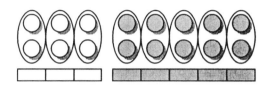

   1 unit = 2 counters.
   The number of yellow counters = 3 units
   The number of red counters = 5 units

   - We can write a ratio for the number of units of yellow counters to the number of units of red counters. We say that the ratio of yellow counters to red counters is the ratio of the units, which is 3 : 5.
   - Tell students that the ratio 3 : 5 does not mean that there are 3 yellow counters and 5 red counters. Here 3 is the number of equal units of yellow counters and 5 is the number of equal units of red counters. When we say that the ratio of yellow counters to red counters is 3 : 5, we mean that for every 3 yellow counters, there are 5 red counters.
   - Ask students for the ratio of red counters to yellow counters. It is 5 : 3. Point out that 5 : 3 is different from 3 : 5. One is the ratio of red counters to yellow counters, and the other is the ratio of yellow counters to red counters.

3. Discuss **tasks 2-6, textbook pp. 72-73**.

4. Discuss finding ratios when measurement is involved.
   - Discuss **tasks 7-9, textbook p. 74**.
   - Point out that when finding the ratio of two measurements, the size of the units has to be the same. That is also true when using ratio to compare two measurements. In task 7, we compared the number of milliliters in both containers. If we have 2 liters of water in one container X, and 1000 ml in container Y, we can't say that the ratio of the volume of water in container X to the volume of water in container Y is 2 : 1000. That would make us think there is much more water in container B than container A. Since 1000 milliliter = 1 liter, the ratio of the volume in X to the volume in Y is 2 : 1.
   - Once we have a ratio, using equal units, what the units are doesn't matter. When we say that the ratio of the weight of package C to package D is 5 : 7, we are saying that for every 5 units of weight in Package C there are 7 units of weight in Package D. The ratio would be the same whether Package C weighed 5 pounds and Package D weighed 7 pounds, or package C weighed 5 grams and Package D weighed 7 grams.

Workbook Exercise 34

Copyright © 2005 SingaporeMath.com Inc., Oregon

| **Part 2: Equivalent Ratios** | **3 sessions** |

Objectives

- Find equivalent ratios.
- Express a ratio in simplest form.
- Use the comparison model to represent a ratio of two quantities.
- Solve word problems involving a ratio of two quantities.

Materials

- Counters or other objects, 2 colors

Homework

- Workbook Exercise 35
- Workbook Exercise 36

Notes

If each term (each number) of a ratio has a common factor, the ratio can be written in simpler terms.

$$8 : 4, 4 : 2, \text{ and } 2 : 1 \text{ are } \textbf{equivalent ratios}.$$

If there is no common factor for all the terms, then the ratio is in its **simplest form**.

$$2 : 1 \text{ is the simplest form of the ratio } 8 : 4.$$

We simplify a ratio by dividing each term of the ratio by its common factors. We can divide 12 and 18 by the common factor 6. We can show this step using cancellation – crossing out the term and writing the quotient.

$$\cancel{12}^{2} : \cancel{18}^{3} = 2 : 3$$

Reducing a ratio to its simplest form can be done in several steps.

$$12 : 18 = 6 : 9 = 2 : 3$$

In the first step the common factor is 2, and in the second it is 3.

Simplification of ratios uses the same process as simplification of fractions. Students will be taught the equivalence of ratios with fractions in Primary Mathematics 6.

Ratios can be diagrammed as unit bars. Since in a ratio two quantities are being compared, we can use a comparison model to illustrate word problems involving ratios. For example, if the ratio of A to B is 5 : 7, this can be diagrammed using 5 units for A and 7 units for B.

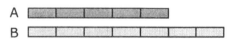

If we are given the value for A, the value for B, the total, or the difference between A and B, we can find the value for 1 unit by division. Once we find the value for 1 unit, we can find other values by multiplication.

Copyright © 2005 SingaporeMath.com Inc., Oregon

Activity 5.2a   **Equivalent ratios**

1. Illustrate equivalent ratios.
   - Provide each student or group of students with counters in two colors. Have them pick out 6 counters of one color and 12 of another. (If you have two-color counters, you can give each student or group 18 counters and have them show one color for 6 of them and the other color for 12 of them.) In this discussion, we use 6 red and 12 yellow counters.
   - Ask students for the ratio of the number of red counters to yellow counters (6 : 12). Then ask for the ratio of the number of yellow counters to red counters (12 : 6).

   - Ask students to put the counters into groups of 2.

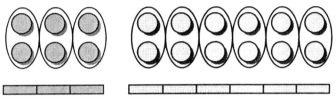

     o Ask for the ratio of the number of units of red counters to units of yellow counters (3 : 6).
     o Point out that 1 unit = 2 counters, and 3 : 6 means 3 units to 6 units. For every 3 red counters, there are 6 yellow counters.

   - Repeat by having your student put the counters in groups of 3, and then in groups of 6. Each time discuss the value of one unit.

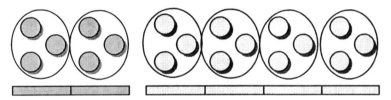

   Ratio of red counters to yellow counters = 2 : 4   1 unit = 3 counters

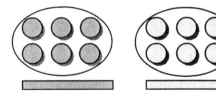

   Ratio of red counters to yellow counters = 1 : 2   1 unit = 6 counters

   - Tell students that we have found four different ratios to compare the number of red counters with yellow counters. These are **equivalent ratios**.

     $$6 : 12 = 3 : 6 = 2 : 4 = 1 : 2$$

   - Ask students how we can derive one equivalent ratio from the other. We can divide each term by a common factor to get a simpler ratio. 2 is a common factor of 6 and 12. 6 ÷ 2 = 3 and 12 ÷ 2 = 6

     $$\cancel{6}^{3} : \cancel{12}^{6} = 3 : 6$$

Copyright © 2005 SingaporeMath.com Inc., Oregon

- Tell students that 1 : 2 is the **simplest form** of the ratio. The terms do not have a common factor (other than 1). The simplest form can be obtained from 6 : 12 by dividing both terms by the common factor 6, or it can be obtained in steps, such as dividing both terms first by the common factor 3, and then by the common factor 2.

$$\not{6}^{1} : \not{12}^{2} = 1 : 2$$

$$\not{6}^{2} : \not{12}^{4} = \not{2}^{1} : \not{4}^{2} = 1 : 2$$

2. Discuss **p. 75** and **tasks 1-3, p. 76** in the **textbook**.

Workbook Exercise 35

Activity 5.2b   **Word problems**

1. Review finding the simplest form for a ratio.
   - Ask students to find the simplest form for the following:

     ➢ Find the ratio of 14 m to 0.77 km   (1 : 55)
     ➢ For the two square shown here, what is the ratio of the perimeter of the larger square to the smaller square? (4 : 3)
     ➢ What is the ratio of the area of the larger square to the smaller square? (16 : 9)
     ➢ What is the ratio of the area of the larger shaded triangle to the smaller shaded triangle? (16 : 9)
     ➢ US: Joan is 4 ft 2 in. tall. Paul is 5 ft 5 in. tall. What is the ratio of Joan's height to Paul's height? (10 : 13)

6 cm

8 cm

1. Discuss **tasks 4-7, textbook pp. 77-78**.
   - Make sure students can relate the information in the diagrams with the information in the word problems. Students should understand how to draw diagrams for ratio problems. Since we are comparing two quantities, we need to draw a separate bar for each quantity. We show the units as the same size. In most ratio word problems, the best approach is to first find the value of 1 unit.
   - Provide some additional problems where students need to draw diagrams on their own, such as the following:
     ➢ The ratio of Mary's age to Carly's age is 4 : 7. The difference in their ages is 6 years. How old is Mary? (8)
     ➢ There were 5 children to every 9 adults at a fair. If there were 420 people (adults and children) at the fair, how many children were there? (150)
     ➢ US: Peter had some quarters and some dimes. The ratio of the value of the quarters to the value of the dimes is 25 : 12. What is the ratio of the number of quarters to the number of dimes? (5 : 6).
       ○ We need to find an equivalent ratio for 25 : 12 where the first term is divisible by 25, the value of a quarter, and the second term is divisible by 10, the value of a dime. Such a ratio would be 250 : 120. This would be the ratio of the value of the coins if we had 10 quarters and 12 dimes. So the ratio of the number of coins is 10 : 12, or 5 : 6.

Workbook Exercise 36

Copyright © 2005 SingaporeMath.com Inc., Oregon

Activity 5.2c   **Practice**

1. Have students do **Practice 5A, textbook p. 79** and share their solutions. Compare different methods they may come up with. Possible solutions for problems 4, 5, and 7 are given here.

    4.   2 units = 4 ℓ

            1 unit = $\dfrac{4}{2}$ = 2 ℓ

            7 units = 2 x 7 = 14 ℓ
            She used 14 ℓ of water.

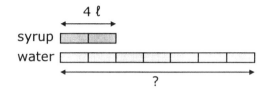

    5.   5 units = 60 m

            1 unit = $\dfrac{60}{5}$ = 12 m

            2 units = 12 x 2 = 24 m
            The shorter piece was 24 m long.

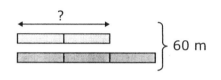

    7.   2 units = 100

            1 unit = $\dfrac{100}{2}$ = 50

            7 units = 50 x 7 = 350
            There are 350 children altogether.

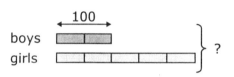

Copyright © 2005 SingaporeMath.com Inc., Oregon

Part 3: Comparing Three Quantities	2 sessions

Objectives

- Compare three quantities using ratios.
- Express a ratio of three quantities in simplest form.
- Solve word problems involving ratios of three quantities.

Materials

- Counters or other objects, 3 colors

Homework

- Workbook Exercise 37
- Workbook Exercise 38

Notes

The concept of ratios, equivalent ratios, and simplest form is extended to the comparison of three quantities in this section.

Given 12 oranges, 18 apples, and 24 bananas, we could write the ratio of oranges to apples to bananas as 12 : 18 : 24. Then we simplify the ratio by dividing the three terms by the common factor 6. The ratio 2 : 3 : 4 shows the *relative* sizes of the number of the three quantities. Students will have to remember that the ratio must show the comparisons in the listed order. If we had asked instead for the ratio of bananas to apples to oranges, that would be 24 : 18 : 12 which, simplified, is 4 : 3 : 2.

Word problems involving ratios comparing three quantities can be solved using diagrams involving units and a comparison model.

Copyright © 2005 SingaporeMath.com Inc., Oregon

Activity 5.3a   **Ratios of three quantities**

1. Discuss the comparison of three quantities, using ratios.
   - Provide each group of students with counters in three colors, such as red, green, and blue. Give them 12 red counters, 24 blue counters, and 18 green counters.
   - Have students write the ratio of red counters to blue counters to green counters. (12 : 24 : 18)
   - Then have students group the counters in equal units (units of 2, 3, and 6) and compare the number of equal units as ratios. (For example, if the counters are grouped in units of 2, the ratio of red counters to blue counters to green counters is 6 groups : 12 groups : 9 groups.)

$$12 : 24 : 18 = 6 : 12 : 9 = 4 : 8 : 6 = 2 : 4 : 3$$

   - Discuss how each equivalent ratio can be obtained from 12 : 24 : 18 by dividing each term by a common factor.
   - Ask students which ratio is in its simplest form (2 : 4 : 3). For every 2 red counters there are 4 blue counters and 3 green counters.
   - Have students write the ratio of green counters to yellow counters to blue counters in both the original numbers and then in simplest form.

2. Discuss **textbook p. 80** and **task 1, textbook p. 81**.

3. Provide some additional practice, such as the following:

   ➢ Simplify the ratios
     - ○ 68 : 36 : 52   (17 : 9 : 13)
     - ○ 42 : 30 : 12   (7 : 5 : 2)
     - ○ 18 : 81 : 63   (2 : 9 : 7)

   ➢ The ratio of the number of swordtails to guppies in an aquarium is 5 : 4. The ratio of the number of guppies to angelfish is 8 : 3.
     - ○ What is the ratio of the number of swordtails to guppies to angelfish? (10 : 8 : 3)
     - ○ What is the ratio of angelfish to the total number of fish? (1 : 7)

     Equivalent ratios need to be found so that the value is the same for the item that is common to both. Find a common multiple for 4 and 8.

swordtails	guppies	angelfish	
5	4		= 10 : 8
8	3		= 8 : 3

   ➢ The ratio of Xenia's savings to Yvonne's savings is 3 : 7. The ratio of Yvonne's savings to Zoe's savings is 3 : 5. What is the ratio of Xenia's : Yvonne's : Zoe's savings? (9 : 21 : 35)

     Find a common multiple for 7 and 3.

Xenia	Yvonne	Zoe	
3	7		= 9 : 21
	3	5	= 21 : 35

Workbook Exercise 37

Copyright © 2005 SingaporeMath.com Inc., Oregon

Activity 5.3b   **Word problems**

1. Discuss **task 2, textbook p. 81**.
   - In word problems involving ratios, we are comparing numbers, so we use a comparison model. We draw unit bars to represent the ratio. The value of each unit bar is the same. Drawing a diagram makes it much easier to solve ratio problems.

2. Provide additional problems. Get students to draw diagrams to solve them.
   - ➢ A string is cut into three pieces in the ratio 5 : 4 : 3. If the longest piece of string is 24 cm longer than the shortest piece of string, what was the total length of the string before it was cut? (144 cm or 1 m 44 cm)
   - ➢ Alice, Betty, and Cassie have $70 altogether. The ratio of Alice's money to Betty's money is 1 : 3. Cassie has $10 more than Alice. What is the ratio of Alice's money to Betty's money to Cassie's money? (6 : 18 : 11)
   - ➢ Charlie, David, and Edward have some toy cars. The ratio of Charlie's cars to David's cars is 4 : 3 and the ratio of David's cars to Edward's cars is 6 : 5. Edward has 6 fewer cars than Charlie. How many cars did they have altogether? (38)

Workbook Exercise 38

Activity 5.3c   **Practice**

1. Have students do **Practice 5B, textbook p. 82** and share their solutions. Compare different methods they may come up with. Possible solutions for problems 4, 6, 7, and 9 are given here.

4.   11 units = 121

   $$7 \text{ units} = \frac{121}{11} \times 7 = 77$$

   There are 77 boys.

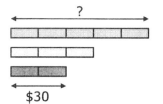

6.   9 units = 90 cm
      1 unit = 90 ÷ 9 = 10 cm

   (a)   3 units = 10 x 3 = 30 cm   (b)   2 units = 10 x 2 = 20 cm
          30 cm was painted green.   20 cm was painted black.

7.   6 units = 24 m^3
      1 unit = 24 ÷ 6 = 4 m^3

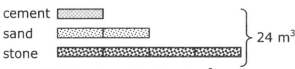

   (a)   1 unit = 4 m^3 (b)   2 units = 4 x 2 = 8 m^3
          4 m^3 cement was used.   8 m^3 sand was used.

9.   2 units = $30

   $$5 \text{ units} = \$\frac{30}{2} \times 5 = \$75$$

   The biggest share is $75.

Copyright © 2005 SingaporeMath.com Inc., Oregon

Unit 6 – Angles

Objectives

- Estimate and measure angles.
- Tell direction in relation to an 8-point compass.
- Find unknown angles involving complementary angles, supplementary angles, angles at a point, and vertically opposite angles.

Suggested number of sessions: 5

	Objectives	Textbook	Workbook	Activities
Part 1 : Measuring Angles				**2 sessions**
61	▪ Estimate and measure angles. ▪ Construct angles of a given size.	p. 83 p. 84, task 1	Ex. 39	6.1a
62	▪ Tell direction in relation to an 8-point compass. ▪ Tell the angle between various points of the compass. ▪ Understand clockwise and counterclockwise turning in relation to an 8-point compass.	p. 84, tasks 2-3	Ex. 40	6.1b
Part 2 : Finding Unknown Angles				**3 sessions**
63	▪ Recognize that vertically opposite angles of intersecting lines are equal. ▪ Recognize that adjacent angles on a straight line add up to 180°. ▪ Recognize that all the angles around a point of intersecting lines add up to 360°.	pp. 85-86		6.2a
64	▪ Find unknown angles involving complementary angles, supplementary angles, angles at a point, and vertically opposite angles.	pp. 87-88, tasks 1-7	Ex. 41	6.2b
65	▪ Practice			6.2c

Copyright © 2005 SingaporeMath.com Inc., Oregon

| Part 1: Measuring Angles | 2 sessions |

Objectives

- Estimate and measure angles.
- Tell direction in relation to an 8-point compass.
- Determine the angle between various points on the compass.

Materials

- Protractors
- Folding meter stick, or other strips attached at the ends
- Compasses (directional)
- Paper circles

Homework

- Workbook Exercise 39
- Workbook Exercise 40

Notes

Students learned how to measure angles in *Primary Mathematics 4A*. This is reviewed and reinforced in this section.

Students should know the size of a right angle (90°), two right angles (180°), three right angles (270°) and four right angles (360°). They should be able to recognize an angle as being about 10°, about 30°, about 45°, and about 60° so that they can estimate the size of other angles which are less than a right angle.

Students will be introduced to the 8-point compass. The angle between any two adjacent points on an 8-point compass is 45°.

Copyright © 2005 SingaporeMath.com Inc., Oregon

Activity 6.1a

1. Review angles.
   - Remind students that angles are a measure of the amount, or degree, of turning from one line to another line with a common point. You can use two pieces of cardboard or plastic connected at one end with a brad, or a folding meter stick, to demonstrate the concept of an angle as an amount of turning.

   - Ask students for the number of degrees in one full turn around a circle (360°). Form a right angle with the strips, a quarter turn, or draw a right angle. Ask for the number of degrees in a right angle (90°).

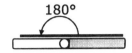

   - Similarly, make sure students know the number of degrees in a half-turn (180°) and a three quarter turn (270°). Have your student tell you the number of right angles in a quarter turn, half turn, three-quarter turn, or full turn.

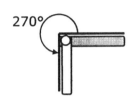

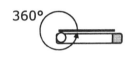

   - Remind students that *angle* is abbreviated with ∠. An angle is named with a lowercase letter, or with three points named with uppercase letters, one on each arm and one at the vertex, with the one at the vertex in the middle.

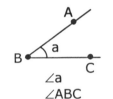

   - Draw a 90 degree angle and then bisect it with a line. Ask students to estimate the size of the angle formed. It is half of 90°, or 45°. Extend the lines for the 45° and ask students if this changes the size of the angle. It does not, since the angle depends on the amount of turning, not the length of the lines.

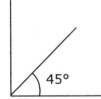

   - Draw another 90 degree angle and divide it into thirds. Ask students to estimate the size of each angle formed. The angles are a third of 90°, which is 30°, and two thirds of 90°, which is 60°.

   - Divide the 30° angle into thirds and mark the 10° angle.

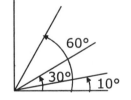

   - Tell students they should be able to recognize angles that are 10°, 30°, 45°, and 60°. They should also be able to recognize a 90° angle, a 180°, and a 270° angle. They can refer to these angles for comparison in visually estimating other angles. For example, an angle that is about a third of the way past 90° would be about a 120° angle.

   - Draw some angles and have your student estimate their measurement. In the example at the right, the angle is about a third of the way past 90° to 180°, and so is about 120°.

Copyright © 2005 SingaporeMath.com Inc., Oregon

2. Review measuring angles less than 180°.
   - Provide students with protractors and have them examine them.
   - Remind them that there are two curves on the protractor, each labeled with the degrees, and each starting at 0° on different sides of the protractor. Only the outer curve has markings between tens, but these markings can be used even when using the inner curve to find the degrees.
   - Demonstrate how to measure some angles less than 180° with a protractor, using a large demonstration protractor or overhead projector. Point out that the vertex of the angle must be placed at the center of the protractor's base line and the base line must be lined up along one of the arms of the angle.
   - Demonstrate how to draw angles less than 180°. First draw a line with the bottom edge of the protractor and mark where the vertex of the angle will be. Line up the vertex with the center of the protractor's base line and the drawn line with the base line. Mark a dot at the appropriate angle. Use the edge of the protractor to connect the vertex with the dot.
   - You can have students practice drawing and measuring angles. They can work in pairs – one student draws an angle for the other student to first estimate and then measure with the protractor.

3. Review measuring angles greater than 180°.
   - Refer to **p. 83** in the **textbook** and discuss the two methods for measuring angles greater than 180°.
     - We can measure the difference from a half-turn, and then add that to 180°.
     - We can measure the opposite smaller angle, and then subtract that from 360°.
   - We would use the same idea to draw angles greater than 180°.
   - Have students practice drawing and measuring angles greater than 180°.

4. Have students do **task 1, textbook p. 84.**
   - Students can trace the angles onto paper so that they can extend the lines to make measuring the angles easier.

Workbook Exercise 39

Activity 6.1b   **Compass angles**

1. Discuss an 8-point compass.
   - Use a compass to find north and have students tell you which direction is south, east, and west.
   - Provide students with a paper circle and have them fold it into eighths by folding it in half, half again, and half again. Have them mark each crease with a line. Guide them in labeling these lines with the eight points of the compass. Have them first mark north, south, east, and west, then north-east, south-east, south-west, and north-west.
   - You may want to discuss the use of these terms in everyday language. For example, show a map and have students tell you what areas on the map are in the south-west of the country.

2. Discuss angles between the points of a compass.
   - Have students use the paper compass they made.
   - Ask students for the angle between each line (45°).
   - Have students compare their paper compass to the face of a clock. Discuss the meaning of going in a clockwise or counterclockwise direction (the 3rd edition uses the term anti-clockwise for counterclockwise).

Copyright © 2005 SingaporeMath.com Inc., Oregon

- Discuss the angles between various points of the compass. For example, ask students for the angle between north and southwest, both in a clockwise direction and a counterclockwise direction.
- Have students stand up and face north. Ask them to point to different directions. ("Where is south-west?")
- Have students turn to a certain compass point, either clockwise or counterclockwise, and then tell you the angle they turned. For example, have them face north and turn clockwise to the south-east. They turned 135°.
- Ask students to face north and then turn 45° counterclockwise, and tell you what direction they are facing (north-west).
- Ask students to face north and then turn 270° clockwise, and tell you what direction they are facing (west).
- Have students stand up again and repeat the activity using different starting positions. For example, have them face west and turn counterclockwise to the north-east. Or, have them face south-west, and tell them to turn 270° clockwise, and give the direction they are now facing (south-east).

3. Have students do **tasks 2-3, textbook p. 84.**

4. Follow directions using angles and compass points.
   - Have students work in pairs. Each student writes a series of commands starting with facing a certain direction followed by four commands to turn a certain number of degrees (multiples of 45° only) clockwise or counterclockwise. The other student has to determine the direction he would be facing after following the commands.

Workbook Exercise 40

Copyright © 2005 SingaporeMath.com Inc., Oregon

| Part 2: Finding Unknown Angles | 2 sessions |

Objectives

- Recognize that vertically opposite angles of intersecting lines are equal.
- Recognize that adjacent angles on a straight line add up to 180°.
- Recognize that all angles around the intersection of lines add up to 360°.
- Find unknown angles involving vertically opposite angles, angles formed by lines intersecting at a point on a straight line, and angles formed by lines intersecting at a point.

Materials

- Protractors

Homework

- Workbook Exercise 41

Notes

In *Primary Mathematics 4A*, students learned that when given a right angle divided into two parts, and the angle of one of those parts, they can find the angle for the other part by finding the difference between the known angle and 90°.

Here they will learn some more angle properties that can be used to find unknown angles involving intersecting lines.

Angles that add up to 90° are called complementary angles and those that add up to 180° are called supplementary angles. It is not a requirement of this curriculum that they memorize those terms at this time.

Copyright © 2005 SingaporeMath.com Inc., Oregon

Activity 6.2a   **Angle properties of lines**

1. Investigate angle properties of lines.
   - Draw two intersecting lines on the board and label the angles formed as a, b, c, and d in order, clockwise.
   - Have each student draw two intersecting straight lines and measure each of their angles. Encourage them not to draw their lines exactly like yours in order to get a variety of angles.
   - Under your drawing of intersecting lines, draw a table on the board with columns labeled $\angle$a, $\angle$b, $\angle$c, and $\angle$d. Have the students tabulate their results in this table.
   - Discuss the results and see if students can come up with some patterns. They should come up with the following:
     - Angles a and c are equal.
     - Angles b and d are equal
     - The sum of angles a and b is 180°, the sum of angles b and c is 180°, the sum of angles c and d is 180°, and the sum of angles d and a is 180°.
     - The sum of angles a, b, c, and d is 360°.
   - Have student do the activities on **p. 86** of the **textbook**. They should measure the angles with their protractors.
   - Have them draw other drawings like those on p. 86 to see if the rules are true for all cases.
   - Remind them that they know one more rule about angles. Draw a right angle and divide it up into two angles. Give the measurement of one angle and ask students what the other angle would be. If a right angle is divided up into two or more parts, the sum of the angles formed is 90°. So in the example at the right, $\angle$x = 90° - 40° = 50°
   - Remind students that a little square drawn in a corner means that the angle is a right angle.

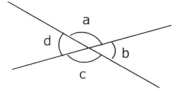

$\angle$a	$\angle$b	$\angle$c	$\angle$d
142	38	142	38

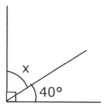

Activity 6.2b   **Find unknown angles**

1. Find unknown angles using angle properties.
   - Discuss **tasks 1-2, textbook p. 87**.
   - Tell students that these figures are not drawn to scale; they are just "rough drawings". So they cannot find the unknown angles by measurement. Instead they need to use the angle properties they have learned to calculate the value of the unknown angles.
   - Have students do **task 3, textbook p. 87** and give reasons for each step of their solution.
   - Discuss **tasks 4-5, textbook p. 88**.
   - Have students do **tasks 6-7, textbook p. 88** and give reasons for each step of their solutions.

Workbook Exercise 41

Copyright © 2005 SingaporeMath.com Inc., Oregon

Activity 6.2c   **Practice**

1. Provide additional practice with finding unknown angles. You can use the problem set on the next page. Students should be able to give reasons for each step of their solutions.

    1.   ∠a = 38°
    2.   ∠b = 43°
    3.   ∠c = 44°
    4.   ∠AEB = 54°
    5.   ∠z = 300°
    6.   ∠EAF = 35°

2. Have students create problems for other students to solve.

Copyright © 2005 SingaporeMath.com Inc., Oregon

Problem Set 6.2c
Figures are not drawn to scale.

1. AB, CD, and EF are straight lines. Find ∠a.

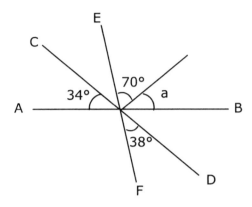

2. AB is a straight line. Find ∠b.

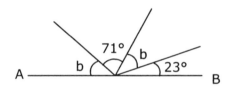

3. Find ∠c.

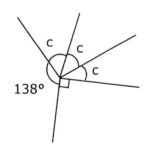

4. AB is a straight line. The ratio of ∠AEB : ∠BEC : ∠CED is 3 : 6 : 1 Find ∠AEB.

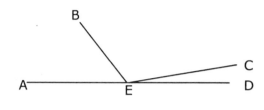

5. ∠z is 12 times as large as ∠x. ∠y is 10° larger than ∠x. Find ∠z.

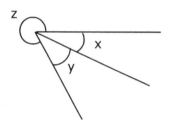

6. ABCD is a rectangle. ∠BAF = 60° and ∠EAD = 65°. Find ∠EAF.

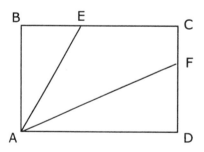

Copyright © 2005 SingaporeMath.com Inc., Oregon

Review

Objectives

- Review all topics.

Suggested number of sessions: 5

	Objectives	Textbook	Workbook	Activities
Review B				**5 sessions**
66				
67	• Review.	pp. 89-92, Review B US edition only: pp. 93-96, Review C	Review 2	R.2
68				
69				
70				

Activity R.2   **Review**

1. Select some of the problems in **Review B, textbook pp. 89-92** and in **Review C, textbook pp. 93-96** (US edition only) to work on as a class. Have students work on the other problems individually. Students should then share their solutions. Possible solutions for some problems are shown here.

Review B

14. 12 units = 1500

$$3 \text{ units} = \frac{1500}{12} \times 3 = 375$$

Or:

$$\frac{3}{10} \times \frac{5}{6} \times 1500 = 375$$

There were 375 [US] single men [[3d] Malaysians].

15. 3 units = $756

$$2 \text{ units} = \$\frac{756}{3} \times 2 = \$504$$

She had $504 left.

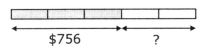

16. 1 unit = Brett's money
Maria's money = 1 unit + $60
4 units = $600 - $60 = $540

$$1 \text{ unit} = \$\frac{540}{4} = \$135$$

$135 + $60 = $195
Maria had $195.

(3d edition: Dan ↔ Ali, Brett ↔ Ramat)

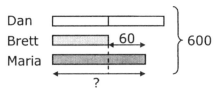

19. 5 units = $180
1 unit = $180 ÷ 5 = $36
John received $36 more than Peter.

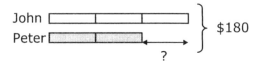

Copyright © 2005 SingaporeMath.com Inc., Oregon

21. 3 units = $30

$1 \text{ unit } = \$\dfrac{30}{3} = \$10$

12 units = $10 x 12 = $120
Total sum of money = $120

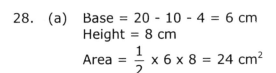

(**3d**> Sean ↔ Sumin, Ryan ↔ Raju)

28. (a) Base = 20 - 10 - 4 = 6 cm
Height = 8 cm

$\text{Area} = \dfrac{1}{2} \times 6 \times 8 = 24 \text{ cm}^2$

(b) Base = 10 cm
Height = 5 cm

$\text{Area} = \dfrac{1}{2} \times 10 \times 5 = 25 \text{ cm}^2$

(c) Area of rectangle = 12 x 24
= 288 cm²
Base of unshaded Δ = 4 cm

$\text{Area of } \Delta = \dfrac{1}{2} \times 4 \times 24$

= 48 cm²
Shaded area = 288 - 48
= 240 cm²

(d) Base = 2 cm
Height = 10 cm

$\text{Area} = \dfrac{1}{2} \times 2 \times 10 = 10 \text{ cm}^2$

Review C

2. $\text{David's weight} = \dfrac{1}{2}(259 - 17)$

= 121 lb

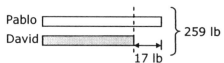

11. length = 5 units = 30 yd
1 unit = 30 ÷ 5 = 6 yd
width = 2 units = 6 yd x 2 = 12 yd
perimeter = 2 x (30 yd + 12 yd) = 2 x 42 yd = 84 yd
area = 30 yd x 12 yd = 360 yd²

20. $\dfrac{2}{3} \rightarrow 6 \text{ c}$

$\dfrac{1}{3} \rightarrow 6 \text{ c} \div 2 = 3 \text{ c}$

$\dfrac{3}{3} \rightarrow 3 \text{ c} \times 3 = 9 \text{ c}$

Or:

6 c

2 units = 6 c
1 unit = 3 c
3 units = 3 c x 3 = 9 c

22. (a) 3 yd 2 ft x 7
= 21 yd 14 ft
= 21 yd + 12 ft + 2 ft
= 21 yd + 4 yd + 2 ft
= 25 yd 2 ft

(b) 5 lb 14 oz x 3
= 15 lb 42 oz
= 15 lb + 32 oz + 10 oz
= 15 lb + 2 lb + 10 oz
= 17 lb 10 oz

(c) 4 gal 3 qt x 5
= 20 gal 15 qt
= 20 gal + 12 qt + 3 qt
= 20 gal + 3 gal + 3 qt
= 23 gal 3 qt

(d) 2 ft 11 in. x 2
= 4 ft 22 in.
= 4 ft + 12 in. + 10 in.
= 4 ft + 1 ft + 10 in.
= 5 ft 10 in.

Copyright © 2005 SingaporeMath.com Inc., Oregon

23. (a)   3 yd 1 ft ÷ 2 = (2 yd + 3 ft + 1 ft) ÷ 2 = (2 yd + 4 ft) ÷ 2 = 1 yd 2 ft

    (b)   2 lb 10 oz ÷ 6 = (32 oz + 10 oz) ÷ 6 = 42 oz ÷ 6 = 7 oz

    (c)   6 gal 3 qt ÷ 3 = (6 gal ÷ 3) + (3 qt ÷ 3) = 2 gal 1 qt

    (d)   2 ft 8 in. ÷ 4 = (24 in. + 8 in.) ÷ 4 = 32 in. ÷ 4 = 8 in.

32. Ashley's weight = 1 unit
    Adding 6 lb will give 1 unit for
    Emily, subtracting (30 – 6) lb
    will give 1 unit for Morgan.
    3 units = 243 + 6 – (30 – 6) = 225
    1 unit = 225 ÷ 3 = 75 lb
    Ashley weighs 75 lb

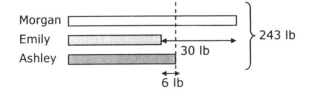

    Or:
    Emily's weight = 1 unit
    Ashley's weight = 1 unit + 6
    Morgan's weight = 1 unit + 30
    3 units + 6 + 30 = 243
    3 units = 243 – 36 = 207
    1 unit = 207 ÷ 3 = 69
    Ashley weighs 75 lb

Copyright © 2005 SingaporeMath.com Inc., Oregon

Textbook Answer Key

Unit 1 - Whole numbers

Part 1: Place Value (pp. 6-7)

1. (a) 20,000 (b) 100,000
2. (a) four hundred thirty-five thousand, six hundred seventy-two
   (b) five hundred thousand, five hundred
   (c) four hundred four thousand, forty
   (d) three hundred forty-five thousand, seven hundred thirteen
   (e) seven hundred thousand, three hundred seventy
   (f) three hundred eleven thousand, twelve
   (g) eight hundred forty thousand, three hundred eighty-two
   (h) six hundred thousand, five
   (i) nine hundred ninety-nine thousand, nine hundred ninety-nine
3. (a) 401,062 (b) 970,505
   (c) 700,009

Part 2: Millions (pp. 8-9)

1. (a) 2 (b) millions
2. (a) five million
   (b) four million, one hundred twenty six thousand
   (c) three million, six hundred ninety thousand
   (d) six million, eight hundred thousand
3. (a) 6,000,000 (b) 7,003,000
   (c) 8,000,000 (d) 9,023,000

Practice A (p. 10)

1. (a) 11,012 (b) 115,600
   (c) 700,013 (d) 880,005
   (e) 5,000,000 (f) 4,200,000
   (g) 10,000,000 (h) 8,008,000
2. (a) two hundred seven thousand, three hundred six
   (b) five hundred sixty thousand, three
   (c) seven hundred thousand
   (d) three million, four hundred fifty thousand
   (e) six million, twenty thousand
   (f) four million, three thousand
3. (a) 800 (b) 80,000 (c) 80
   (d) 800,000 (e) 8000
   (f) 8,000,000

4. (a) 6000 (b) 200,000
   (c) 184,900 (d) 7,609,000
   (e) 9,021,000 (f) 30,000
5. (a) 44,668; 45,668
   (b) 73,500; 74,500
   (c) 103,002; 113,002
   (d) 5,652,000; 5,662,000
   (e) 7,742,000; 5,742,000
6. (a) 53,607; 53,670; 53,760; 56,370
   (b) 324,468; 324,648; 342,468; 342,486
   (c) 425,700; 2,357,000; 2,537,000; 3,257,000

Part 3: Approximation and Estimation (pp. 11-13)

1. 490
2. (a) 600 (b) 800 (c) 1000
3. 5700
4. (a) 3700 (b) 6000 (c) 5000
5. 17,000
6. (a) 23,000 (b) 55,000
   (c) 40,000
7. (b) 74,000 (c) 804,000
   (d) 130,000
8. 600
9. (a) 33,000 (b) 37,000
   (c) 28,000 (d) 700
10. 18,000
11. 700
12. (a) 12,000 (b) 87,000
    (c) 4000 (d) 39,000
    (e) 36,000 (f) 50,000
    (g) 800 (h) 900

Practice 1B (p. 14)

1. (a) 70 (b) 660 (c) 1290
2. (a) 300 (b) 1300 (c) 20,800
3. (a) 7000 (b) 11,000
   (c) 125,000
4. $800
5. $70,000
6. 1,000,000 km
7. (a) Town A: 180,000
       Town B: 176,000
       Town C: 171,000
   (b) 527,000
8. (a) 37,000 (b) 30,000
   (c) 38,000 (d) 48,000
9. (a) 36,000 (b) 54,000
   (c) 900 (d) 600

Copyright © 2005 SingaporeMath.com Inc., Oregon

Part 4: Multiplying by Tens, Hundreds, or Thousands (pp. 15-16)

1. (a) 3280   (b) 53,600
   (c) 63,000
3. (a) 1440   (b) 14,400
   (c) 144,000
4. (a) 27,000   (b) 270,000
   (c) 2,700,000
5. (a) 100,000 (b) 540,000
   (c) 4,800,000
   (d) 1,000,000   (e) 2,400,000
   (f) 10,000,000
6. 14,000
8. (a) 15,000   (b) 32,000
   (c) 480,000

Part 5: Dividing by Tens, Hundreds, or Thousands (pp. 17-18)

1. (a) 52   (b) 74   (c) 40
3. (a) 7   (b) 80   (c) 40
4. 70
6. (a) 80   (b) 70   (c) 9

Part 6: Order of Operations (pp. 19-20)

1. (a) 10   (b) 24   (c) 23
   (d) 32   (e) 147 (f) 99
   (g) 99   (h) 11   (i) 75
2. (a) 64   (b) 5   (c) 27
   (d) 432   (e) 3   (f) 12
   (g) 700   (h) 1   (i) 81
3. (a) 27   (b) 23 (c) 184
   (d) 30   (e) 46 (f) 18
   (g) 20   (h) 134   (i) 0
   (j) 18   (k) 22 (l) 62
4. 11
5. (a) 276   (b) 126 (c) 0
   (d) 180   (e) 10   (f) 459
6. (a) 5   (b) 14
   (c) 29   (d) 20
   (e) 28   (f) 100

Practice 1C (p. 21)

1. (a) 2380   (b) 70,000
   (c) 37,000
   (d) 4000   (e) 28,000
   (f) 520,000
2. (a) 3920   (b) 39,200
   (c) 392,000
3. (a) 6750   (b) 67,500
   (c) 675,000
4. (a) 9000   (b) 900   (c) 90

5. (a) 1500   (b) 150   (c) 15
6. (a) 4   (b) 190   (c) 151
   (d) 51   (e) 700   (f) 103
7. (a) 56   (b) 300
   (c) 3   (d) 15
   (e) 37   (f) 68
   (g) 37   (h) 10
   (i) 21   (j) 70
   (k) 50   (l) 4
8. (a) 356   (b) 356
   (c) 298   (d) 298
   (e) 16   (f) 16
   (g) 64   (h) 64

Part 7: Word Problems (pp. 22-24)

1. 155
2. 936
3. 9
4. 40

Practice 1D (p. 25)

1. 71 kg
2. 48
3. 38 kg
4. $15
5. 40
6. 170
7. $42
8. $10
9. $5
10. $35

Unit 2 - Multiplication and Division by a 2-digit Whole Number

Part 1: Multiplication (pp. 26-27)

1. (a) 3180   (b) 19,760
2. (a) 4640   (b) 2300   (c) 2430
   (d) 12,420 (e) 29,560
   (f) 44,870
3. (b) 2444
   (c) 17,550 (d) 44,496
4. (a) 2948   (b) 2544
   (c) 2784
   (d) 19,352   (e) 15,995
   (f) 28,482
5. (a) 120,510   (b) 313,386
6. (a) 162,127   (b) 440,510
   (c) 121,776
   (d) 266,340   (e) 364,458
   (f) 405,668

Copyright © 2005 SingaporeMath.com Inc., Oregon

Part 2: Division (pp. 28-31)

1. (a) 2 r10   (b) 7 r10
    (c) 4 r9   (d) 8 r65
2. (a) 1 r40   (b) 1 r39   (c) 2 r25
    (d) 7 r50   (e) 6 r73   (f) 7 r18
5. (a) 3 r12   (b) 2 r2   (c) 2 r9
    (d) 2 r8   (e) 2 r8   (f) 1 r28
    (g) 2 r15   (h) 6 r5   (i) 7 r91
    (j) 9 r20   (k) 4 r55   (l) 4 r7
8. (a) 4   (b) 3 r2   (c) 2 r28
    (d) 3 r20   (e) 1 r41   (f) 5
11. (a) 9   (b) 6 r2   (c) 6
    (d) 8 r60   (e) 8   (f) 6 r82
13. (c) 14 r45   (d) 40 r12
14. (a) 23   (b) 22 r22   (c) 20 r5
    (d) 12 r27   (e) 10 r38   (f) 20 r14
15. (c) 106 r36 (d) 70 r35
16. (a) 239   (b) 133 r15 (c) 33 r10
    (b) 107 r16 (d) 28 r18   (e) 340 r4

Practice 2A (p. 32)

1. (a) 34,188   (b) 33,810
    (c) 68,693
2. (a) 275,145   (b) 629,340
    (c) 194,796
3. (a) 3 r17   (b) 2 r26   (c) 3 r2
4. (a) 53   (b) 6 r1   (c) 9 r28
5. (a) 19   (b) 38 r21   (c) 23 r33
6. (a) 98 r40   (b) 58 r6   (c) 179 r4
7. 432
8. 16 ℓ
9. 28
10. $56
11. $59,824
12. $35,064
13. 42
14. $105

Unit 3 - Fractions

Part 1: Fraction and Division (pp. 33-35)

1. $2\frac{3}{4}$

2. $2\frac{2}{3}$

3. 3; 11; $2\frac{3}{4}$

4. (a) $2\frac{1}{3}$ (b) $2\frac{4}{5}$

    (c) $3\frac{1}{2}$ (d) $8\frac{5}{9}$

Practice 3A (p. 36)

1. (a) $2\frac{3}{5}$ (b) 7

    (c) $2\frac{2}{3}$ (d) $8\frac{1}{3}$

2. (a) $3\frac{3}{4}$ (b) $5\frac{1}{4}$

    (c) $3\frac{1}{2}$ (d) $11\frac{1}{7}$

3. $3\frac{1}{4}$ m

4. $\frac{1}{3}$ m

5. $2\frac{1}{2}$

6. $\frac{2}{5}$ ℓ

7. $2\frac{1}{5}$ m

8. $\frac{2}{3}$ kg

Part 2: Addition and Subtraction of Unlike
   Fractions (pp. 37-39)

    $\frac{5}{6}$

1. 9; 4; 13
2. 10; 6; 16; $1\frac{1}{15}$

3. 21; 25; 46; 23; $1\frac{8}{15}$

4. (a) $1\frac{11}{18}$ (b) $1\frac{1}{6}$ (c) $1\frac{2}{15}$
5. 21; 4; 17
6. 25; 3; 22; 11
7. 30+21; 25; 51; 25; 13
8. (a) $\frac{8}{15}$ (b) $\frac{3}{4}$ (c) $\frac{4}{15}$

Practice 3B (p. 40)

1. (a) $1\frac{5}{12}$ (b) $1\frac{1}{15}$ (c) $1\frac{17}{24}$

2. (a) $\frac{1}{4}$ (b) $\frac{2}{15}$ (c) $\frac{7}{12}$

3. (a) $\frac{7}{15}$ (b) $\frac{3}{4}$ (c) $\frac{13}{24}$

4. (a) $\frac{19}{24}$ (b) $\frac{19}{30}$ (c) $\frac{7}{15}$

5. $\frac{13}{20}$

6. $\frac{1}{2}$ hour

Copyright © 2005 SingaporeMath.com Inc., Oregon

7. (a) $\frac{3}{8}$ (b) $\frac{1}{8}$

8. (a) $\frac{17}{20}$ (b) $\frac{3}{20}$

Part 3: Addition and Subtraction of Mixed Numbers (pp. 41-42)

(a) 29; $5\frac{5}{24}$ (b) 16; 4; $6\frac{1}{3}$

1. 5; 27; 32; $5\frac{1}{15}$

2. 2; $1\frac{1}{6}$

3. (a) 21; $1\frac{11}{18}$

    (b) 5; 35; 26; $2\frac{13}{15}$

Practice 3C (p. 43)

1. (a) $4\frac{2}{9}$ (b) $3\frac{23}{24}$ (c) $4\frac{1}{12}$

2. (a) $2\frac{1}{2}$ (b) $2\frac{1}{2}$ (c) $3\frac{7}{12}$

3. (d) $4\frac{7}{18}$ (e) $8\frac{1}{3}$ (f) $4\frac{5}{24}$

4. (a) $2\frac{1}{2}$ (b) $1\frac{1}{15}$ (c) $2\frac{2}{15}$

5. $1\frac{1}{10}$ km

6. $1\frac{1}{2}$

7. $1\frac{1}{4}$ ℓ

8. $\frac{5}{12}$ hours

9. $1\frac{5}{12}$ m

Part 4: Product of a Fraction and a Whole Number (pp. 44-47)

          8
1. (a) $\frac{10}{3}$ (b) $\frac{10}{3}$

2. $7\frac{1}{2}$ $7\frac{1}{2}$ $7\frac{1}{2}$

3. 10

4. (a) 30   (b) 700   (c) 400
    (d) 300   (e) 9   (f) 10
    US (g) 2   US (h) 4   US (i) 3

5. 45 min; 2 h 45 min

6. (a) 2 h 20 min
    (b) US 4 yd 2 ft   3d 4 min 40 s
    (c) US 5 gal 1 qt   3d 5 m 25 cm

(d) 3 km 500 m
(e) 14 ℓ 900 ml
(f) 6 years 3 months

7. 400 m; 3400 m

8. 48 h; 6 h; 54 h

9. (a) 250
    (b) US 24   3d 1900
    (c) US 14   3d 84
    (d) 33
    (e) 1300   (f) 260
    (g) 2100   (h) 200
    (i) US 69   3d 575

10. (a) $\frac{2}{5}$ (b) $\frac{3}{5}$ (c) $\frac{3}{10}$

    (d) $\frac{3}{4}$ (e) $\frac{5}{12}$

Practice 3D (p. 48)

1. (a) 7   (b) $6\frac{1}{2}$ (c) 16

2. (a) 24   (b) $26\frac{2}{3}$ (c) $8\frac{1}{3}$

3. (a) 49   (b) 52   (c) 45

4. (a) 40 min   (b) 600 g

5. (a) 80 cm   (b) 900 m

6. (a) 8 years 9 months
    (b) 3 ℓ 600 ml

7. (a) US 9 lb 4 oz   3d 9 kg 250 g
    (b) 5 h 20 min

8. (a) US 42 in.   3d 350 cm
    (b) US 17 qt   3d 255 min

9. (a) 2,700 m   (b) 112 h

10. (a) $\frac{9}{10}$ (b) $\frac{3}{8}$ US (c) $\frac{1}{4}$

11. (a) $\frac{3}{4}$ (b) $\frac{5}{12}$ US (c) $\frac{1}{3}$

12. $\frac{10}{11}$

13. $\frac{1}{5}$

Part 5: Product of Fractions (pp. 49-51)

1. $\frac{3}{10}$

2. $\frac{9}{20}$

3. $\frac{5}{18}$

4. $\frac{1}{12}$

5. $\frac{8}{15}$

Copyright © 2005 SingaporeMath.com Inc., Oregon

6. $\frac{3}{8}$

7. (a) $\frac{1}{4}$ (b) $\frac{1}{4}$ (c) $\frac{2}{9}$

   (d) $\frac{1}{6}$ (e) $\frac{5}{8}$ (f) $\frac{3}{10}$

   (g) $\frac{5}{18}$ (h) $\frac{2}{7}$ (i) $\frac{7}{12}$

   (j) 10 (k) 12 (l) $5\frac{1}{3}$

Practice 3E (p. 52)

1. (a) $\frac{1}{8}$ (b) $\frac{5}{18}$ (c) $\frac{3}{8}$

2. (a) $\frac{1}{5}$ (b) $\frac{2}{3}$ (c) $\frac{3}{4}$

3. (a) $\frac{1}{3}$ (b) $\frac{1}{2}$ (c) $\frac{1}{4}$

4. (a) 12 (b) $2\frac{2}{3}$ (c) 4

5. (a) 5 (b) 4 (c) 5

6. $\frac{1}{6}$ m

7. US $\frac{3}{10}$ qt   3d $\frac{3}{10}$ ℓ

8. $\frac{3}{5}$ kg

9. $\frac{1}{6}$

10. $\frac{3}{8}$ m²

Part 6: Dividing a Fraction by a Whole Number (pp. 53-54)

1. $\frac{2}{9}$

2. (a) $\frac{1}{8}$ (b) $\frac{1}{15}$

   (c) $\frac{1}{5}$; $\frac{1}{6}$ (d) $\frac{1}{3}$; $\frac{3}{10}$

3. (a) $\frac{1}{6}$ (b) $\frac{4}{15}$ (c) $\frac{5}{28}$

   (d) $\frac{1}{5}$ (e) $\frac{3}{7}$ (f) $\frac{1}{12}$

   (g) $\frac{3}{16}$ (h) $\frac{1}{16}$ (i) $\frac{3}{20}$

Practice 3F (p.55)

1. (a) $\frac{1}{9}$ (b) $\frac{5}{18}$ (c) $\frac{3}{10}$

2. (a) $\frac{3}{20}$ (b) $\frac{1}{20}$ (c) $\frac{4}{27}$

3. (a) $\frac{2}{15}$ (b) $\frac{1}{9}$ (c) $\frac{1}{12}$

4. $\frac{2}{5}$ m

5. $\frac{1}{5}$

6. $\frac{1}{20}$ kg

7. $\frac{1}{10}$ pt [ℓ]

8. $\frac{3}{16}$ m

9. $\frac{1}{8}$ kg

Part 7: Word Problems (pp. 56-59)

    75
1. 36
2. 20
3. 480
4. 60
5. 50
6. $1000

Practice 3G (p. 60)

1. 42
2. $70
3. $180
4. 40
5. 24
6. 192
7. (a) $\frac{3}{16}$ (b) $3200
8. 46

Review A (pp. 61-64)

1. (a) 515,407   (b) 4,600,000
2. (a) eight hundred seventy-two thousand, five hundred twenty
    (b) one million, thirty-four thousand
    (c) four million, five hundred thousand
    (d) one hundred sixty-two thousand, three
3. 9,000,000
4. 5,164,000
5. (a) $438,000   (b) 43,000 km
6. 281,000
7. $2,356,000
8. (a) 1, 2, 4, or 8
    (b) Any multiple of 40
9. (a) 5000   (b) 35,000
    (c) 3000   (d) 8000

Copyright © 2005 SingaporeMath.com Inc., Oregon

10. 4200; 6000
11. (a) 21,000   (b) 300,000
     (c) 700   (d) 90
12. (a) 1,590,000   (b) 4,980,000
     (c) 2,752,000
     (d) 16   (e) 16 r10   (f) 12
13. (a) 1008   (b) 3900
     (c) 19,680
     (d) 14   (e) 24   (f) 12 r13
14. (a) 79   (b) 54
     (c) 22   (d) 32
     (e) 23   (f) 9
     (g) 40   (h) 9
15. (a) $\frac{3}{4}$ (b) $\frac{3}{5}$
     (c) $\frac{2}{3}$ (d) $\frac{4}{5}$
16. (a) $\frac{43}{8}$ (b) $\frac{40}{11}$
     (c) $\frac{41}{9}$ (d) $\frac{11}{4}$
17. (a) $3\frac{1}{3}$ (b) $4\frac{1}{2}$
     (c) 11   (d) $3\frac{3}{4}$
18. (a) $\frac{6}{8}, \frac{9}{12}, \frac{12}{16}...$
     (b) $\frac{1}{3}, \frac{4}{12}, \frac{6}{18}...$
     (c) $\frac{10}{18}, \frac{15}{27}, \frac{20}{36}...$
     (d) $\frac{22}{28}, \frac{33}{42}, \frac{44}{56}...$
19. (a) $\frac{2}{3}$ (b) $\frac{5}{18}$
     (c) $3\frac{1}{2}$ (d) $2\frac{6}{7}$
20. (a) $\frac{3}{2}$ (b) $2\frac{1}{2}$ (c) 4
     (d) $1\frac{6}{7}$ (e) $4\frac{2}{3}$ (f) $\frac{16}{5}$
21. (a) $1\frac{5}{8}, 1\frac{3}{4}, \frac{9}{4}, \frac{9}{2}$
     (b) $1\frac{2}{8}, 1\frac{2}{3}, \frac{8}{2}, \frac{36}{5}$
22. $\frac{7}{9}$
23. 13
25. (a) $1\frac{7}{12}$ (b) $3\frac{19}{24}$ (c) $8\frac{3}{10}$
     (d) $5\frac{1}{7}$ (e) $4\frac{1}{12}$ (f) $3\frac{11}{15}$
25. (a) $1\frac{2}{5}$ (b) 15   (c) 14

     (d) $\frac{2}{3}$ (e) $\frac{7}{12}$ (f) $\frac{8}{15}$
     (g) $\frac{1}{5}$ (h) $\frac{7}{16}$ (i) $\frac{1}{21}$
26. (a) 60 cm   (b) 1 kg 700 g
   US (c) 2 lb 12 oz
27. (a) $\frac{1}{3}$ (b) $\frac{8}{15}$ US (c) $\frac{1}{7}$
28. 25
29. 354
30. 45 cm
31. $347
32. 192
33. $1120
34. $\frac{7}{8}$
35. $\frac{7}{10}$ kg
36. 18
37. $1\frac{1}{2}$ ℓ
38. $\frac{3}{20}$ kg
39. $\frac{1}{8}$
40. (a) $\frac{2}{5}$ (b) $1500
41. 2 m
42. 896

Unit 4 - Area of Triangle

Part 1: Finding the Area of a Triangle (pp. 65-70)

1. (a) 24   (b) 40   (c) 60
2. (a) 20 cm²
     (b) US 54 in.²   3d 54 cm²
     (c) $31\frac{1}{2}$ m²
     (d) US 220 ft²   3d 220 m²
3. (a) US 630 yd²   3d 630 m²
     (b) 96 cm²
     (c) 42 m²   (d) 15 cm²
4. (a) 120 cm²   (b) 36 m²
5. (a) 68 cm²   (b) 240 m²
     (c) 224 cm²

Practice 4A (p. 70)

1. A 21 cm²   B 22 cm²
   C 36 m²   D 49 m²
2. 150 cm²

Copyright © 2005 SingaporeMath.com Inc., Oregon

3. 144 cm^2
4. (a) 63 cm^2
   (b) 5104 m^2

Unit 5 – Ratio

Part 1: Finding Ratio (pp. 71-74)

1. 1 : 3
2. 2 : 3
3. 2 : 5; 5 : 2
4. 3 : 2
5. 3 : 7
6. 5 : 4
7. 4 : 6
8. 3 : 8
9. 5 : 7

Part 2: Equivalent Ratios (pp. 75-78)

1. (a) 2 : 5   (b) 2 : 3
2. (a) 4 : 5   (b) 5 : 3
   (c) 1 : 4   (d) 3 : 2
3. 5 : 4
4. 5 : 3
5. 3; 12; 12
6. 5; 20; 20
7. 8; 64; 64

Practice 5A (p. 79)

1. (a) 1 : 2   (b) 3 : 2
2. 4 : 3
3. 7 : 3
4. 14 ℓ
5. 24 m
6. 40 kg
7. 350

Part 3: Comparing Three Quantities (pp. 80-81)

   (a) 2 : 1
   (b) 6 : 3 : 2
1. (a) 6 : 3 : 2
   (b) 4 : 2 : 3
2. 2; 10; 10

Practice 5B (p. 82)

1. 5 : 12
2. 12 : 4 : 7
3. 4 cups
4. 77
5. 5 : 6

6. (a) 30 cm   (b) 20 cm
7. (a) 4 m^3 (b) 8 m^3
8. 102 kg
9. $75

Unit 6 - Angles

1 Measuring Angles (pp. 83-84)

1. 123º
2. 240º
3. 325º
2. (a) 135º   (b) 45º
3. (a) north-east   (b) north-west

Part 2: Finding Unknown Angles (pp. 85-88)

   146; 34; 146
   85; 45; 180
   150; 150; 360
1. (a) 48   (b) 143   (c) 345
2. x = 134º; y = 46º; z = 134º
3. ∠COB = 155°
4. ∠DBE = 90°
5. ∠x = 35°
6. ∠m = ∠n = 40°
7. ∠a = 29°   ∠b = 145°   ∠c = 85°

Review B (pp. 89-92)

1. 19,000
2. $43,000

3. (a) 6700   (b) 72,800
   (c) 350,000 (d) 430
   (e) 580   (f) 628
4. 24
5. $\frac{4}{15}$
6. $\frac{1}{4}$
7. 2 h 15 min
8. 60 cm
9. (a) $105   (b) $80   (c) $165
10. 3 m
11. $\frac{1}{10}$ m
12. 48
13. $1\frac{1}{5}$ kg
14. 375
15. $504
16. $195

Copyright © 2005 SingaporeMath.com Inc., Oregon

17. $45
18. $57
19. $36
20. 300 m²   70 m
21. $120
22. 14 cm
23. (a) 44 m 84 m²
    (b) 58 cm   140 cm²
24. (a) ∠a = 160°
    (b) ∠b = 205°
25. (a) ∠x = 207°
    (b) ∠x = 47°
26. (a) 75 cm² (b) 42 cm² (c) 18 cm²
27. 54 m²
28. (a) 24 cm² (b) 25 cm²
    (c) 240 cm² (d) 10 cm²

US Review C (pp. 93-96)

1. 5800 mi
2. 121 lb
3. 5 qt
4. $1\frac{1}{4}$ ft
5. 0.8 qt or $\frac{4}{5}$ qt
6. $10\frac{2}{3}$ oz
7. 1728 in³
8. (a) $\frac{1}{6}$ (b) $\frac{3}{8}$ (c) $\frac{1}{2}$
9. 9 in.
10. $4\frac{4}{5}$ lb
11. 84 yd   360 yd²

12. (a) 42 ft 68 ft²
    (b) 40 in.   69 in.²
13. 2 gal 4 c
14. 1.74 ft
15. 36 in.
16. 12 oz
17. (a) 1 ft 6 in. (b) 2 ft 4 in.
    (c) 4 ft 9 in.
18. 216 in.³
19. 504 ft³
20. 9 cups
21. 10 qt 2 c
22. (a) 25 yd 2 ft
    (b) 17 lb 10 oz
    (c) 23 gal 3 qt
    (d) 5 ft 10 in.
23. (a) 1 yd 2 ft
    (b) 0 lb 7 oz
    (c) 2 gal 1 qt
    (d) 0 ft 8 in.
24. 4 ft 6 in.
25. (a) 8 yd
    (b) 28 in. (2 ft 4 in.)
    (c) 21 oz (1 lb 5 oz)
    (d) 10 gal
26. 8 lb 5 oz
27. 3.7 mi
28. 0.46 lb
29. $5.65
30. 258.8
31. 37 in.
32. 75 lb

Copyright © 2005 SingaporeMath.com Inc., Oregon

Workbook Answer Key

Exercise 1

1. (a) 24,608   (b) 16,011
   (c) 99,009   (d) 312,460
   (e) 802,003   (f) 540,014
   (g) 900,909
2. (a) Fifty thousand, two hundred thirty-four
   (b) Twenty-six thousand, eight
   (c) Seventy-three thousand, five hundred six
   (d) Three hundred sixty-seven thousand, four hundred fifty
   (e) Five hundred six thousand, nine
   (f) Four hundred thirty thousand, sixteen
   (g) Eight hundred thousand, five hundred fifty
3. (a) 7000   (b) 6; 60,000
   (c) hundreds   (d) 40
4. (a) 42,108   (b) 562,032
   (c) 770,077   (d) 900,214
5. (a) 800   (b) 300,000
   (c) 3000   (d) 8
6. (a) 36,552; 37,552
   (b) 71,880; 72,080
   (c) 30,361; 31,361
7. (a) 31,862   (b) 42,650
   (c) 33,856   (d) 65,703
8. 96,431; 13,469; 87,611; 11,678

Exercise 2

1. (a) 3,000,000   (b) 4,150,000
   (c) 6,031,000   (d) 7,208,000
   (e) 5,005,000   (f) 9,909,000
   (g) 10,000,000
2. (a) Four million
   (b) Three million, forty thousand
   (c) Six million, three hundred fifty thousand
   (d) Five million, six thousand
   (e) Seven million, seven hundred three thousand
   (f) Nine million, ninety-nine thousand
   (g) Eight million, five hundred sixty-seven thousand
3. $2,003,705   Two million, three thousand, seven hundred five dollars
4. $2,400,000   Two million, four hundred thousand dollars

Exercise 3

1. (a) 300   (b) 1320
2. (a) 6000   (b) 36,300
3. (a) 46,000   (b) 236,000
4. (a) 245,000   (b) 248,000
5. (a) 43,190   (b) 14,600
   (c) 83,000   (d) 196,000
6. (a) $4400   (b) $5300
   (c) $26,100   (d) $39,700
   (e) $59,900   (f) $62,300
7. (a) $3000   (b) $6000
   (c) $18,000   (d) $25,000
   (e) $44,000   (f) $49,000
   (g) $329,000   (h) $693,000

Exercise 4

1. (a) 36,000   (b) 13,000
   (c) 40,000
2. (a) 49,000   (b) 4000
   (c) 39,000
3. (a) 1600   (b) 2000
   (c) 12,000
4. (a) 300   (b) 300   (c) 800
5. (a) 9000   (b) 13,000
   (c) 32,000   (d) 96,000
   (e) 3000   (f) 4000
   (g) 28,000   (h) 62,000
6. (a) 6000   (b) 20,000
   (c) 48,000   (d) 50,000
   (e) 2000   (f) 800
   (g) 1000   (h) 700

Exercise 5

1. (a) 2540   (b) 60,200
   (c) 3720   (d) 57,000
   (e) 25,800   (f) 313,600
   (g) 360,000   (h) 2,415,000
2. (a) 15,000   (b) 48,000
   (c) 21,000   (d) 200,000
3. $6000
4. ^{US} 9000 in.^{2} ^{3d} *9000 cm^2*

Exercise 6

1. (a) 36   (b) 42
   (c) 5   (d) 7
   (e) 15   (f) 15
   (g) 7   (h) 16
2. (a) 6   (b) 8
   (c) 90   (d) 60

Copyright © 2005 SingaporeMath.com Inc., Oregon

3. $30
4. 30 m

Exercise 7

1. (a) 97   (b) 17
    (c) 35   (d) 34
    (e) 280   (f) 8
    (g) 42   (h) 40
2. (a) 132   (b) 20
    (c) 50   (d) 85
    (e) 62   (f) 83
    (g) 115   (h) 108
3. (a) 70   (b) 1
    (c) 115   (d) 100
    (e) 33   (f) 12
    (g) 59   (h) 9

Exercise 8

1   (a) 100   (b) 30
    (c) 34   (d) 3
    (e) 48   (f) 42
    (g) 36   (h) 1
2. (a) 7   (b) 60
    (c) 32   (d) 100
    (e) 30   (f) 8
    (g) 12   (h) 100
3. (a) 24   (b) 46
    (c) 336   (d) 30
    (e) 65   (f) 4
    (g) 10   (h) 38

Exercise 9

1. 16
2. $100
3. 124
4. $84

Exercise 10

1. $24
2. $6
3. $54
4. $32

Exercise 11

1. (a) 3120   (b) 2300
    (c) 1272   (d) 5785
    (e) 17,220   (f) 18,540
    (g) 16,256   (h) 66,120
2. (a) 37,710   (b) 280,560
    (c) 37,400   (d) 80,977

(e) 85,600   (f) 63,189
(g) 78,475   (h) 377,522

Exercise 12

1. (a) 3   (b) 3 r4
    (c) 9 r70   (d) 6 r37
    (e) 3 r2   (f) 1 r39
    (g) 9 r4   (h) 5 r34
2. (a) 5 r7   (b) 3 r19
    (c) 3 r2   (d) 2 r28
    (e) 5 r51   (f) 8 r21
    (g) 7 r47   (h) 5 r2

Exercise 13

1. (a) 17 r18   (b) 20 r20
    (c) 15 r7   (d) 13
    (e) 32 r5   (f) 33 r7
    (g) 19 r22   (h) 16 r12
2. (a) 243   (b) 517 r10
    (c) 120   (d) 318 r7
    (e) 82   (f) 92 r25
    (g) 162 r25   (h) 120 r8

Review 1

1. (a) Two thousand, forty-four
    (b) Fifteen thousand, five hundred eight
    (c) Three hundred seventy-six thousand,
        nine hundred twenty
    (d) Six million, four hundred thousand
2. (a) 4008   (b) 27,300
    (c) 60,011   (d) 2,904,000
3. (a) 58,030   (b) 6,042,500
4. (a) 4   (b) 10,000
5. (a) 7206   (b) 63,440
    (c) 40   (d) 800
6. (a) 45,832   (b) 30,012
7. 87,660; 76,435; 64,748; 60,083
8. (a) 1, 2, 3, 4, 6, 8, 12, 24
    (b) 6, 12, 18, 24, 30, 36,
        42, 48, 54, 60, 66, 72
9. 80,999
10. (a) 45   (b) 76
    (c) 301   (d) 382
11. (a) 294   (b) 305
    (c) 5500   (d) 2; 50   (e) 2; 6
12. (a) 49,500   (b) 50,000
13. (a) 12,999   (b) 2021
    (c) 15,120
    (d) quotient - 3   remainder - 7
14. (a) 160   (b) 120
15. 200 cm²

Copyright © 2005 SingaporeMath.com Inc., Oregon

16. (a) 64 cm^2 (b) 36 cm

17.

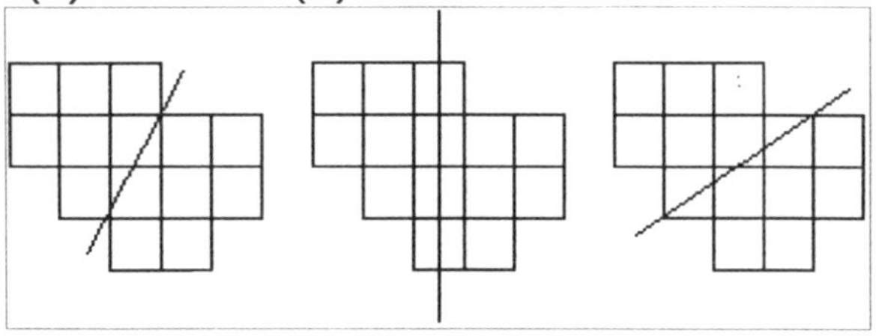

18. (a) US 15 $in.^2$ 3d *15 cm^2*
    (b) US 18 in. 3d *18 cm*
19. $230
20. $75
21. 158
22. $1500

Exercise 14

1. (a) $\frac{3}{2}$ (b) $\frac{5}{3}$ (c) $\frac{7}{4}$
2. $2\frac{2}{3}$, $3\frac{1}{3}$, $2\frac{2}{5}$, $2\frac{3}{4}$, $4\frac{3}{5}$, $6\frac{2}{3}$
3. (a) 4 (b) $2\frac{1}{5}$
   (c) $2\frac{1}{8}$ (d) 9

Exercise 15

1. (a) $1\frac{5}{8}$ (b) $1\frac{1}{9}$ (c) $1\frac{1}{10}$
   (d) $1\frac{1}{3}$ (e) $1\frac{1}{2}$ (f) $1\frac{2}{5}$
2. (a) $\frac{11}{12}$ (b) $1\frac{1}{18}$ (c) $1\frac{1}{10}$
   (d) $1\frac{3}{20}$ (e) $1\frac{1}{15}$ (f) $1\frac{2}{15}$

Exercise 16

1. (a) $\frac{1}{8}$ (b) $\frac{3}{4}$ (c) $\frac{2}{5}$
   (d) $\frac{1}{4}$ (e) $\frac{3}{4}$ (f) $\frac{1}{2}$
2. (a) $\frac{3}{10}$ (b) $\frac{5}{24}$ (c) $\frac{9}{20}$
   (d) $\frac{3}{20}$ (e) $\frac{8}{15}$ (f) $\frac{14}{15}$

Exercise 17

1. (a) $3\frac{7}{8}$ (b) $4\frac{3}{4}$ (c) $6\frac{1}{10}$
   (d) $5\frac{1}{12}$ (e) $5\frac{1}{3}$ (f) $4\frac{1}{2}$
2. (a) $3\frac{13}{15}$ (b) $4\frac{13}{24}$ (c) $7\frac{3}{20}$
   (d) $6\frac{5}{18}$ (e) $4\frac{7}{15}$ (f) $5\frac{11}{15}$

Exercise 18

1. (a) $2\frac{3}{8}$ (b) $3\frac{7}{10}$ (c) $2\frac{1}{4}$
   (d) $4\frac{1}{6}$ (e) $1\frac{4}{9}$ (f) $2\frac{5}{6}$
2. (a) $3\frac{5}{18}$ (b) $2\frac{1}{12}$ (c) $2\frac{1}{18}$
   (d) $2\frac{11}{24}$ (e) $1\frac{5}{12}$ (f) $\frac{7}{15}$

Exercise 19

1. (a) 15 (b) 70
   (c) 27 (d) US $3\frac{1}{4}$ 3d *750*
   (e) 9 (f) 900
   (g) 600 (h) 50
2. (a) 2; 60 (b) 4; 700
   (c) 3; 15 (d) 2; 12
   (e) 2; 400 (f) 5; 250
   (g) US 4; 12 3d *4; 750*
   (h) 3; 875

Exercise 20

1. (a) 2100 (b) 70
   (c) 32 (d) 3500
   (e) 2200 (f) 170
   (g) 460 (h) 3800
2. 3125 m
3. US Pablo, 20 min
   3d *Hassan, 20 min*
4. (a) $1\frac{1}{2}$ ℓ
   (b) the same 3d *105 min*
   (c) 2500 m
   (d) 120 cm
   US (e) $1\frac{3}{4}$ ft.
5. (a) $1\frac{1}{4}$ ℓ (b) 30 h
   (c) US the same 3d *18 mths*
   (d) 1400 g US (e) $2\frac{1}{4}$ qt

Exercise 21

1. $\frac{2}{3}$

Copyright © 2005 SingaporeMath.com Inc., Oregon

2. $\frac{19}{20}$

3. $\frac{3}{4}$

4. $\frac{3}{20}$

5. $\frac{13}{20}$

6. $\frac{1}{3}$

7. US $\frac{2}{9}$ 3d $\frac{1}{4}$

8. $\frac{3}{10}$

9. (a) $\frac{3}{8}$ (b) $\frac{5}{8}$

Exercise 22

1. (a) $\frac{1}{10}$ (b) $\frac{3}{8}$

    (c) $\frac{1}{3}$ (d) $\frac{4}{9}$

2. (a) $\frac{2}{9}$ (b) $\frac{3}{32}$

    (c) $\frac{3}{20}$ (d) $\frac{5}{9}$

    (e) $\frac{1}{2}$ (f) $\frac{2}{15}$

    (g) $\frac{3}{4}$ (h) $\frac{9}{28}$

Exercise 23

1. $\frac{5}{6}, \frac{1}{9}, \frac{3}{8}, \frac{1}{12}, \frac{3}{40}, \frac{2}{3}, \frac{1}{2}, \frac{2}{5}$

2. US $\frac{5}{9}$ lb   3d $\frac{5}{9}$ kg

3. US $\frac{3}{10}$ yd²   3d $\frac{3}{10}$ m²

4. $\frac{2}{15}$

Exercise 24

1. (a) $\frac{1}{8}$ (b) $\frac{1}{6}$

    (c) $\frac{2}{9}$ (d) $\frac{1}{10}$

2. (a) $\frac{3}{8}$ (b) $\frac{2}{9}$

    (c) $\frac{1}{6}$ (d) $\frac{1}{15}$

    (e) $\frac{2}{5}$ (f) $\frac{5}{42}$

(g) $\frac{5}{24}$ (h) $\frac{2}{45}$

Exercise 25

1. (a) $\frac{5}{3}$ $\frac{5}{6}$

         $\frac{5}{9}$ $\frac{10}{3}$ $\frac{5}{6}$

    (b) $\frac{1}{6}$ $\frac{2}{3}$

         $\frac{1}{9}$ $\frac{1}{12}$ $\frac{1}{12}$

2. US $\frac{1}{10}$ lb   3d $\frac{1}{10}$ kg

3. US $\frac{1}{10}$ yd   3d $\frac{1}{10}$ m

4. $\frac{1}{6}$

Exercise 26

1. 35
2. $100
3. $48
4. 126

Exercise 27

1. US 200 gal   3d 200 ℓ
2. 100
3. $320
4. $100

Exercise 28

1. 30
2. $90
3. 40
4. 4 kg

Exercise 29

1. 1000
2. 400
3. $70
4. $16

Exercise 30

2. (a) BC   (b) DF   (c) QR
    (d) YZ   (e) LN   (f) RT

Exercise 31

1. (a) 66 cm²   (b) 44 m²
    (c) 70 cm²   (d) 50 m²

Copyright © 2005 SingaporeMath.com Inc., Oregon

2. (a) 15 cm²   (b) 30 m²
   (c) 135 cm²   (d) 150 cm²

Exercise 32

1. (a) ᵁˢ 36 in.²   ³ᵈ *36 cm²*
   (b) ᵁˢ 90 in.²   ³ᵈ *90 cm²*
   (c) ᵁˢ 112 yd²   ³ᵈ *112 m²*
   (d) ᵁˢ 180 yd²   ³ᵈ *180 m²*
2. (a) ᵁˢ 120 in.²   ³ᵈ *120 cm²*
   (b) ᵁˢ 70 in.²   ³ᵈ *70 cm²*
   (c) ᵁˢ 91 ft²   ³ᵈ *91 m²*
   (d) ᵁˢ 220 ft²   ³ᵈ *220 cm²*
3. A - 18 cm²   B - 36 cm²
   C - 15 cm²   D - 45 cm²
   E - 18 cm²
   (a) D   (b) C
   (c) 30 cm²   (d) B
   (e) A & E

Exercise 33

1. (a) 96 cm²   (b) 30 cm²
   (c) 48 m²   (d) 27 m²
2. (a) 42 cm²   (b) 48 cm²
   (c) 420 m²   (e) 240 m²

Exercise 34

1. (a) 3 : 4   (b) 4 : 3
2. (a) 5 : 3   (b) 3 : 5
3. (a) 2 : 3   (b) 3 : 2
4. (a) 5 : 3   (b) 3 : 5
5. (a) 3 : 7   (b) 7 : 3
6. (a) 6 : 5   (b) 5 : 6

Exercise 35

1. (a) 2 : 5   (b) 3 : 5
2. 2 : 3   3 : 1
   1 : 4   3 : 5
   5 : 3   2 : 1
   5 : 6   4 : 5
   1 : 2   5 : 4
3. (a) 5   (b) 32   (c) 36
   (d) 28   (e) 1   (f) 2
   (g) 1   (h) 12   (i) 4
   (j) 15   (k) ᵁˢ $1\frac{1}{4}$ or 1.25   ³ᵈ *1*
   (l) 4
4. 5 : 4
5. 3 : 2
6. 13 : 18

Exercise 36

1. 105
2. 112 cm
3. $40
4. $112

Exercise 37

1. 2 : 4 : 3
2. 3 : 2 : 4
3. 3 : 1 : 4
4. 6 : 5 : 4
5. 4 : 3 : 5
6. 3 : 3 : 2

Exercise 38

1. 180
2. 20 cm

Exercise 39

1. a = 38°   b = 65°
   c = 90°   d = 121°
   e = 160°   f = 180°
   g = 202°   h = 245°
   i = 270°   j = 307°
   k = 338°   l = 360°
2. a = 66°   b = 230°
   c = 128°   d = 335°

Exercise 40

1. south; north-east; south-east; west; north-west; east; south-west
2. north-east; east; south-east; north-west; 45°; 90°; 135°; 45°

Exercise 41

1. a = 45°   b = 58°
   c = 48°   d = 336°
   e = 110°   f = 90°
   g = 152°   h = 145°
2. q = 28°   r = 117°   s = 77°
   t = 101°   u = 50°

Review 2

1. (a) ᵁˢ <   ³ᵈ *smaller than*
   (b) ᵁˢ <   ³ᵈ *smaller than*
   (c) ᵁˢ =   ³ᵈ *equal to*
   (d) ᵁˢ >   ³ᵈ *greater than*

Copyright © 2005 SingaporeMath.com Inc., Oregon

2. (a) $2\frac{23}{24}$ (b) $2\frac{4}{9}$

   (c) $\frac{7}{12}$ (d) 20

3. (a) 4, 30   (b) 2, 3
   (c) 3, 90   (d) 5, 300

4. (a) 85 cm   (b) $1\frac{2}{3}$ year

   (c) $2\frac{1}{10}$ kg (d) 3 ℓ 50 ml

5. $\frac{3}{8}$

6. US 81 yd²   3d $81\ m^2$

7. 900

8. 896

9. $120

10. 3, 9

11. 16

12. (a) US 12 in.   3d $12\ cm$
   (b) US 240 in.²   3d $240\ cm^2$
   (c) US 64 in.   3d $64\ cm$

13. (a) 6 cm   (b) 33 cm
14. (a) 68°   (b) 142°
15. $\frac{1}{3}$

16. (a) 65 kg   (b) 52 kg
17. 10 m
18. $2\frac{1}{2}$, $\frac{9}{4}$, $2\frac{1}{12}$, $\frac{12}{11}$

19. $3\frac{11}{12}$

20. (a) US 42 in.²   3d $42\ cm^2$
   (b) US $97\frac{1}{2}$ ft²   3d $97\frac{1}{2}\ m^2$

21. 432 m²
22. $50
23. $2400
24. US 20 in.   3d $20\ cm$

Copyright © 2005 SingaporeMath.com Inc., Oregon